Making Thirteen Colonies 1600–1740

TEACHING GUIDE FOR THE REVISED 3RD EDITION

For Elementary School Classes

Oxford University Press
Oxford   New York
Auckland   Bangkok   Buenos Aires
Cape Town   Chennai   Dar es Salaam   Delhi   Hong Kong   Istanbul
Karachi   Kolkata   Kuala Lumpur   Madrid   Melbourne   Mexico City   Mumbai
Nairobi   São Paulo   Shanghai   Singapore   Taipei   Tokyo   Toronto

and an associated company
Berlin

Published by Oxford University Press, Inc.
198 Madison Avenue, New York, New York 10016
Oxford is a registered trademark of Oxford University Press

ISBN 978-0-19-976735-9

Writer: Karen Edwards
Editor: Rosely Himmelstein
Editorial Consultant: Susan Buckley

Printed in the United States of America on acid-free paper

NOTE FROM THE AUTHOR

Dear Teacher,

Every writer of history has to make decisions. Most of those decisions are about what to leave out. It would take libraries and libraries of books to include all of America's history (and there would still be things left out).

So there are all kinds of stories about America (and its heroes and villains and ordinary people) that are not in this book. I see that as an opportunity for you and your students. Tell them the author is upset about what she had to omit. Have them do their own chapters of *A History of US*. Maybe you can do a class volume. Consider focusing on family stories: what can each of your students find out about his or her ancestors? Or maybe you'll want to do a book about your community with chapters on people and organizations and past events.

I have fun tracking down stories; I think you and your students will, too. (Yes, I hope you'll become a student with them.) Writing history is a lot like being a detective or a newspaper reporter. It involves searching for information, digesting it, and then using it. There are hardly any better skills for this Information Age of ours.

You and your students might want to find out more about Indians—especially the Native Americans in the region where you live. Or more about Coronado, or Ben Franklin, or about Americans not even mentioned in these books. Good writers look for details. Check paintings and photographs. What does your subject look like? How did he or she dress? What was daily life like for that person?

You might want to produce the work in comic book form, or write it as a play, or create a ballad. The big idea here is to "do" history, as you might do art or music. At its best, it's a creative activity.

But the big reason I wrote these books was to teach reading and, when it comes to critical reading, history shines. Few subjects give you real events and real people to discuss and analyze. Literacy exercises and paragraph analysis may help some students, but there is nothing like reading a whole book—tracing its ideas from chapter to chapter, and then talking about the ideas—to make a mind work.

This learning guide has words to study and maps to look at and questions to answer. You may want your students to do all the activities, or you may want them to do just a few. Some activities are for those who want to go beyond the text.

Will all this help students pass standardized tests? You bet. Just to be sure, though, I have added some pages with names and dates that you may ask students to memorize.

But there are things in history more important than memorized dates. History is a thinking subject, and you have Information Age kids as your charge. Doing history means reading, researching, finding information, and making connections. If you want to stretch young minds, history will make it happen.

Joy Hakim

CONTENTS

ABOUT THIS TEACHING GUIDE

A History of US is the story of what happened in the United States to the people who live here—both before and after the country got its name. In *Making Thirteen Colonies*, students will learn what happened between 1600 and 1740. This teaching guide, containing strategies and assessment suggestions as well as a range of activities for enrichment and extension, was prepared to help you guide your students through the book.

FOCUSING ON FREEDOM

The cornerstone of American history is Freedom. It is the idea that pulsates throughout *A History of US:* the hunger for freedom, the fight for freedom, the legislating of freedom, the protection of freedom, the defense of freedom. As you teach this volume of *A History of US*, students will learn how the accomplishments of people, the force of ideas, and the outcome of events are all linked in this nation's great story of Freedom.

A lot happens: sad, exhilarating, unexpected, disappointing, terrible, puzzling, inspiring things. And many people are involved: the wise, the misguided, the brave, the reckless, the patient, the bullies, the compromisers. It's a grand and sweeping story.

May you and your students enjoy it together.

THE TEACHING UNITS

Each book of *A History of US* has been divided into units of study that we call Parts. Each Part consists of chapters that have a common focus. The Teaching Guide provides strategies and activities that you can use to teach each Part.

- **Part 1: Planting Colonial Seeds** (Chapters 1-6) focuses on the attempts of early English colonists to settle along the Virginia coast.

- **Part 2: The Seeds Take Root** (Chapters 7-12) focuses on the settlement of Virginia and conflict with the Powhatans.

- **Part 3: Colonizing Massachusetts** (Chapters 13-16) focuses on the early colonization of New England and colonists' relations with the Wampanoag.

- **Part 4: Growing Discontent in New England** (Chapters 17-23) focuses on the religious conflict that helped spread colonization in New England and violent conflict between English colonists and Native Americans.

- **Part 5: Founding the Middle Colonies** (Chapters 24-29) focuses on the founders of the Middle Colonies, trade in the Middle Colonies, and some of the reasons for English colonization in America.

- **Part 6: Founding the Southern Colonies** (Chapters 30-36) focuses on the people and events involved in the settlement of the Southern colonies.

- **Part 7: The Colonies Continue Expanding** (Chapters 37–After Words) focuses on the westward expansion of settlement, the expansion of trade, and the expansion of colonists' ideas of freedom.

ORGANIZING INFORMATION

The history of the United States is rich, busy, and populated. You can help your students organize information and reinforce learning by frequently asking these questions:

- What were the major events?
- Who were the significant people?
- What were the important ideas?

✓ **Question Chart** In every lesson plan, you will see a reference to the Question Chart (Resource 1, TG page 72), on which students may record their answers to these questions as they progress through the book.

THE BIG THEMES

Underlying the events and people and ideas that enliven this series are certain themes—themes that run through human experience and help us make sense of the past.

Among these themes are Justice, Conflict, Independence, Change, Diversity, Adaptation, Growth, and Power. You may wish to post these themes on the walls of your classroom and refer to them at appropriate times. They may also stir students' thinking throughout the course of their study.

Book 2 of *A History of US* focuses on three Big Themes: **Change, Diversity,** and **Conflict.** These themes—and how they relate to this nation's quest for and preservation of freedom—provide the conceptual framework of *Making Thirteen Colonies*.

Among the dramatic changes occurring in the period 1600-1740 are:

- change in the lives and lands of Native Americans.
- change in the attitude of colonists toward people who practiced different religions.
- change in the relationship of the colonies to one another.
- change in the economic power of the colonies.

Among the examples of diversity in this period are:

- Native Americans and colonists learn from each other.
- colonists come from other parts of Europe, and, eventually, Africa.
- people of different religions come to the colonies.

Among the major conflicts in this period are:

- conflicts between Native Americans and colonists.
- conflicts between the idea of a single religion and the idea of religious tolerance.
- conflicts between those who endorsed slavery and those who opposed it.
- conflicts among colonies.

TEACHING STRATEGIES

The Teaching Strategies in this guide are organized in the following manner:

Introducing the Part lays out goals for teaching, sets up a relationship between the Part and the major themes, and seeks to stimulate students' interest as they begin to read the text.

Chapter Lesson Plans are designed to provide you with the flexibility that your individual schedule, interests, and students' abilities may require. You may choose from the following categories:

- **Ask:** straightforward questions to elicit from your students responses that demonstrate their recall and understanding of the text.

- **Discuss:** critical thinking questions to stimulate classroom and/or small-group discussions.

- **Write:** topics for classroom or homework assignment, allowing students to express their comprehension or impressions of the chapter's events, ideas, or people.

- **Ponder:** questions that give students the opportunity to reflect on the thematic material of the chapter, often relating it to their own lives.

- **Literacy Links:** *Words to Discuss,* exploring the chapter's significant vocabulary words or terms, and *Reading Skills* designed to help students develop reading skills, especially for reading nonfiction.

- **Skills Connection:** chapter-related activities to strengthen geography skills, chart/graph skills, study skills, and cross-curricula skills.

- **Meeting Individual Needs:** activities that address the needs of students with differing learning abilities.

Which of these categories will be suitable for your students on any particular day? How many items will be useful to engage your class—or a particular student? The lesson plans have been structured with the belief that *you* are the best person to make these decisions.

Summarizing the Part provides guidance for synthesizing the Part's Big Themes. This guidance consists of a series of questions—which you can use for assessment or discussion—that enable students to deepen their understanding of how the events, ideas, trends, and personalities of the Part reflect common themes. The Part Summary also provides additional Projects and Activities.

PART CHECK-UPS

The reproducible Check-Ups review the content of each Part.

RESOURCES

The Resources are reproducible blackline masters. They cover social studies skills (including maps, graphic organizers, tables, primary sources, and other enrichment materials), critical thinking skills, and reading comprehension skills.

LITERACY AND *A HISTORY OF US*

In our Information Age, reading is an essential survival skill. So what does this have to do with us historians and history educators? We have the key to the nation's reading crisis, and we've been ignoring it: When it comes to critical reading, history shines. Hardly anything approaches it in its demands for analysis and thinking.

Joy Hakim

Teaching with *A History of US* gives you an unparalleled opportunity to focus on literacy. As the author has noted, "Nonfiction is the literary form of our time." Joy Hakim's highly readable nonfiction is a unique tool for teaching strategic reading skills.

READING STRATEGIES AND SKILLS

In order to help your students get the most out of their reading, the Teaching Guides include activities that focus on reading skills as well as reading strategies.

Reading Skills deal with what students actively do with the nonfiction text. The Reading Skills activities in the chapter lesson plans help students identify, evaluate, interpret, understand, and use the following nonfiction elements:

- Text Structure: main idea/supporting details, sequence, comparing and contrasting, question and answer, cause and effect

- Text Features: margin notes, special sections, captions, headings, typeface

- Visual Aids: photographs, paintings, illustrations, political cartoons

- Graphic Aids: graphs, tables, charts, timelines

- Maps: political, physical, historical, special purpose

- Point of View: author's voice and opinion

- Source Material: primary and secondary sources

- Rhetorical Devices: word choice, imagery, connotation/denotation, persuasion, fact and opinion, analogy

Reading Strategies are the intellectual strategies necessary for readers to use their reading skills. Following the ideas of reading authority Janet Allen, these can be categorized as follows:

- Questioning: creating questions to aid with previewing, recalling, and deeper understanding of the text

- Predicting: focusing and guiding reading by previewing text elements and posing questions to be answered

- Visualizing: identifying and using language and imagery to infer, make connections to the text, and predict

- Inferring: identifying text clues and background knowledge to make inferences; using inferences to make predictions and draw conclusions

- Connecting: making personal connections to the text, seeing connections between texts, seeing connections between world events and the text

- Analyzing: recognizing the relationship between author's intention and author's words, determining author's purpose, understanding how parts of the text work together, using material from the text to support response to the text

- Synthesizing: creating an original idea, new line of thinking, or other new creation by combining related ideas

Each Reading Skill activity is related to one of the Reading Strategy categories.

NOTE You probably present material to your students in a variety of ways. There are times you may read aloud to the class or in small groups. Perhaps you'll find it best to have volunteers read aloud—or have the class read silently. You'll find that *A History of US* allows you to vary your approach to suit your schedule and your goals.

LITERACY HANDBOOK: *READING HISTORY*

Reading History is written by Janet Allen, one of American's most prominent literacy advocates. Engaged in the blossoming campaign to integrate literacy and history, Allen provides valuable strategies for teaching nonfiction, taking all examples directly from *A History of US*. Allen says:

> For the past several years, many content teachers have voiced a common complaint: As we teach and learn with a generation of children who have been raised on technology and sophisticated media, it becomes increasingly difficult to entice them Into reading content textbooks. Reading History *has been written to help you teach your students effective strategies for reading* A History of US *as well as other nonfiction. It is filled with practical ideas for making reading history accessible for even your most reluctant readers.*

ASSESSMENT AND *A HISTORY OF US*

Author Joy Hakim intentionally omits from her books the kinds of section, chapter, and unit questions that are used to review and assess learning in standard textbooks. It is her purpose to engage readers in learning—and loving—history. Rather than interrupt student reading, all assessment instruments for *A History of US* appear in the Teaching Guides.

IN THE TEACHING GUIDES

Ask, Discuss, and Write sections in each chapter lesson plan check students' understanding of chapter content.

Summarizing the Part includes questions for discussion or writing, and activities that help students identify major concepts and themes.

Check-Up pages review content for each Part. These are reproducible pages that appear at the end of each Teaching Guide.

Puritan colonist

HISTORICAL OVERVIEW

We . . . having undertaken . . . a voyage to plant the first colony in the northern parts of Virginia, do . . . solemnly and mutually . . . covenant and combine ourselves together into a civil body politic. . . .

In this pledge the Pilgrims declared their intention to found a colony that would be ruled by laws they themselves passed. The document was written on board the *Mayflower* in November 1620, before the 102 English colonists set foot on land. The Mayflower Compact marked a milestone in the making of the 13 English colonies.

English colonizing had begun 13 years earlier, in Virginia, where, in 1607, about 120 colonists settled at Jamestown, making this the first permanent English settlement in America.

The Pilgrims were soon joined by another group seeking religious freedom, the Puritans. Together the Pilgrims and many more Puritans began the settlement of the New England Colonies. From Massachusetts, settlers fanned out to form the colonies of Rhode Island, Connecticut, and New Hampshire.

At the same time, settlers poured into the Middle Colonies. The Dutch colonized New Netherland, but in 1664, the English took control of this area and founded their own colonies there—New York and New Jersey. A few years later, William Penn founded Pennsylvania. Delaware, earlier a part of Pennsylvania, completed the Middle Colonies.

Meanwhile, the Southern Colonies, led by Virginia, were also developing. Maryland was another colony that sprang from religious persecution in England. North and South Carolina followed, founded by proprietors who wanted to profit from land rents and sales. Georgia, established as a refuge for the inmates of English debtors' prisons, brought to thirteen the number of England's colonies in what was to be the United States.

The growth of colonies came at the expense of the First Americans. Through land purchase, treaty, or just plain land-grabbing, European colonists drove the Native Americans off their traditional lands, killing them or forcing them farther west.

Growth of the colonies demanded large supplies of labor. Indentured servants sent from England, by choice or involuntarily, were bound to a master for a few years. A much larger labor force of enslaved Africans was brought to the Southern Colonies where they often made up more than half a colony's population.

The American colonial period sowed the seeds of American ideals, such as freedom of religion, representative government, and equality of opportunity. But it also sowed seeds of future conflicts: between the new Americans and the First Americans; between those for and against slavery; between the North and the South.

Making Thirteen Colonies tells the fascinating story of America's early development.

Metacom, leader of the Wampanoag people

TEACHING STRATEGIES FOR BOOK TWO

Planting Colonial Seeds

The first colonial seeds were ideas planted in people's minds. The ideas came from ancient civilizations—good ideas about exploration and democracy, bad ideas like slavery and intolerance. The next "seeds" were actual people who came to North America and faced overwhelming challenges. They paid a high price for their inexperience and poor planning.

SETTING GOALS

The goals for students in Part 1 are to:
- understand that the new American culture flowed from ancient civilizations.
- identify reasons for the English colonizing effort at Jamestown.
- understand the achievements of the Woodland Indians who inhabited land taken by the colonists.
- describe the key figures in the colonization of Virginia.

GETTING INTERESTED

1. Write the title of Part 1 on the chalkboard. Remind students that seeds are small things from which larger things grow. Ask: what grew from the first colonies in America? *(the United States)* Ask: If we think of the first colonies as seeds, what was required for their survival in an unfamiliar land? *(food, shelter, protection from danger)*

2. Have students leaf through Chapters 1-6, looking at titles, headings, illustrations, captions, margin notes, and quotations. Help students identify maps, portraits, diagrams, margin notes and full pages about topics related to the text. Help students understand that the story of the colonies will be told through people. Ask: Who are some of the subjects in the portraits and illustrations showing people? *(Native Americans, Englishmen, John Smith, Pocahontas)*

⧗ Working with Timelines

Have students start a chronological timeline on which to record significant events and dates from 1600 to 1740. Alternative timelines can focus on an individual life (John Smith), a community (Jamestown), or a topic (slavery). Direct students to the Chronology of Events, on page 170. Discuss what was happening in places other than Jamestown during the years 1607-1610.

🌐 Using Maps

Have students locate on the world map (pages 180-181) the places mentioned in the Preface *(Our Mixed-Up Civilization)*: Iraq, Israel, Egypt, Greece, Spain, the Mediterranean Sea. Then have them look at all the maps in the Atlas (pages 180-186) and discuss the kinds of information each map gives.

A Sign in the Sky

The enormous political, scientific, economic, and religious changes in 17th-century Europe, symbolized by the appearance of a comet in 1607, resulted in Europeans setting out to establish colonies on the North American continent.

ASK

1. What was the "Sign in the Sky?" referred to in the chapter title? *(a comet)* Why were people in Europe in 1607 afraid of it? *(They didn't understand what it was.)*

2. What changes in England and Spain made people afraid in 1607? *(the Queen of England had died, Puritans were in power; Spain was bankrupt)*

3. Who was Galileo? *(an Italian scientist)*

4. Galileo agreed with Copernicus on his idea about the earth and the sun. What was that idea? *(the sun is the center of our universe)*

5. Why did that idea get Galileo in trouble? *(At that time, people believed the earth was the center of the universe; they didn't accept new ideas easily.)*

Ponder
The author says: "Change is troublesome, especially to those in power." What kinds of changes would be especially troublesome to those in power?

Question Chart

DISCUSS

1. Joy Hakim explains in this chapter how hard it was for people long ago to accept new ideas. Ask students if they have ever been faced with a new idea that was difficult to accept. Why was it hard? Did they eventually accept it?

2. Read the last sentence of Chapter 1 aloud, "Pack a bag, we're going to join them." Ask students why this sentence is included at this point in the book? *(Joy Hakim wants readers to get involved in the story by imagining they are part of it.)*

3. Ask students to list three items they would take on a trip into the unknown. Suggest categories of items: for example, food, clothing, entertainment.

WRITE

It is the 17th century. Have students write a letter to Galileo, inviting him to visit their class. They should explain why they would like him to come and what they would like to ask him.

L I T E R A C Y   L I N K S

Words to Discuss

comet   epidemic
superstition

Have students use a dictionary and context to determine the meanings of the words. Discuss: Which word is a synonym for *old wives' tale*? *(superstition)* Which usually describes an illness rather than the spread of ideas? *(epidemic)* Ask students to make a word web with *comet* at the center. Have them write words and concepts related to *comet* in the outer circles.

Reading Skills
Comparing Charts

Have pairs of students look at the two charts of the universe—Copernicus's on page 15 and the contemporary one on page 17. Ask: How many planets did Copernicus include? *(seven)* How many planets are on the modern chart? *(nine)* Besides being in different languages, what is the main difference between the two charts? *(The planets' orbits and distances from the sun are more accurate in the modern chart.)* CONNECTING

Skills Connection
Mathematics

Based on information given in the caption on page 17, challenge interested students to determine the 30 dates that Halley's comet has appeared in Earth's skies since 467 B.C.E.

Across the Ocean

A group of 105 hopeful colonizers—more than half of them gentlemen unused to hard work—sailed from England in 1606 to establish a colony in Virginia.

ASK

1. Have students look at the world map on pages 180-181. What separates Europe and North America? *(Atlantic Ocean)* Look at the map and consider the following questions: How could people cross the ocean in 1607? *(by ship)* How would you cross the ocean today? *(by ship or by airplane)*

2. How long was the trip across the Atlantic from England to Virginia expected to take in 1607? *(six or eight weeks)* How far did the Virginia settlers get in six weeks *(just out of sight of England)*

3. What did the Englishmen who set sail for Virginia in 1606 expect to find there to make them rich? *(gold)*

◎ **Ponder**
Why is gold so desirable that people will take incredible risks to get it? What are some of the things you value most?

✓ **Question Chart**

DISCUSS

1. Read the quote on page 18 and discuss why people believed such an obvious exaggeration. *(People wanted to believe in a place where gold and jewels were easy to find.)*

2. What conditions in England made people consider leaving for a new life somewhere else? *(England seemed crowded; timber and farmland were becoming scarce; the streets were filled with beggars)*

3. Who were "younkers"? Who do you think was responsible for a younker's safety? *(Boys on a ship who climbed rigging, set sails, and kept a lookout for land; they had to look out for themselves.)* Read the last paragraph on page 19 and discuss possible answers to the questions posed by Joy Hakim.

WRITE

Ask students to imagine they are reporters traveling to Virginia with the 105 Englishmen. Ask them to write a headline and a one-paragraph news story about an incident on the trip.

L I T E R A C Y   L I N K S

Words to Discuss

younker   privateer
rigging

Have students use a dictionary as well as the context of Chapter 2 to determine the meanings of the words. Discuss: What is jargon? *(special "insider" words that relate to an occupation or topic)* Which of these words would be considered jargon? *(younker, rigging)* How is *privateer* related to *pirate*? *(A privateer was a pirate licensed by the government.)*

Reading Skills
Understanding Point of View

Joy Hakim hints at what she thinks are the Englishmen's chances of success in America in 1606. Ask students to look at the text for clues. Create a class list of what she says about the travelers—and how she reveals her opinion. *(She doesn't have confidence in their success. She writes: they " were not "expected or trained to work"; "they lived on family money"; most brought their best clothes— puffed knee pants, silk stockings, feathered hats.)* INFERRING

Skills Connection
Geography

Display a map of the world. Explain that students are going to measure the length of the trip taken by English settlers on their voyage in 1606-1607. Have students use the map's scale to estimate the distance from England to the Canary Islands *(about 1,800 miles)*, from the Canary Islands to Martinique *(about 3,000 miles)*, and from Martinique to Virginia *(about 2,000 miles)*.

The First Virginians

A well-organized Woodland Indian culture—farmers and hunters—had long-thrived on the land that would be called Virginia.

ASK

1. Who was the Powhatan? *(the ruler or emperor of five Indian tribes in eastern Virginia)*
2. What was the most important food of Powhatan's people? *(corn)*
3. What did Algonquian boys and girls do together? *(played running games)* What did they do separately? *(boys learned to hunt; girls made pots, helped their mothers)*
4. Why were deer important to the Powhatans? *(deer provided both food and clothing)*

⊚ Ponder
Why is it misleading to call Powhatan's people "The First Virginians?"

✓ Question Chart

DISCUSS

1. What does the muskrat story (page 24) tell you about the Powhatan as a ruler? *(It showed he appreciated the truth, was understanding, and had a sense of humor.)*
2. What was the prophecy given to the Powhatan by his priests and how did he interpret it? *(The priests said his empire would be destroyed by men from the east. Powhatan thought they meant the Chesapeakes, the easternmost of his tribes.)*
3. What problems did overhunting cause the Powhatans? *(Deer became scarce in their territory; they risked war with other tribes if they expanded their hunting grounds.)*

WRITE

Imagine you are a young Woodland Indian. Write a diary entry for the year 1600 describing a typical day.

LITERACY LINKS

Words to Discuss

opossum   raccoon
scarecrow

Have students use a dictionary as well as context to determine the meanings of the words. Discuss: Which words were adopted into English from Algonquian languages? *(raccoon, opossum)* Which word is made up of a verb and a noun that explain what the word means? *(scarecrow)*

Reading Skills
Using Primary Sources

Have students read the margin note Earthly Paradise on page 21 and examine the map on page 23. Ask students what evidence they can find in the map that illustrates the truth of Ralph Lane's description in his letter. *(The map shows many trees and names of Indian tribes.)* ANALYZING

Meeting Individual Needs
English Language Learners

Students may have difficulty pronouncing Indian names and words in this chapter. Have the class work together to create a pronunciation chart. Have students add to it throughout the year.

English Settlers Come to Stay

The settlers who came expecting to find riches found troubles instead—Indian attack, poor location for their settlement, poor policy from their sponsor (the London Company), disease, and starvation.

ASK

1. Why didn't local Indians want Europeans around? *(bad experience with Spaniards who tried to start colonies and who kidnapped an Indian prince)*
2. How did the Englishmen who arrived in 1607 decide who would be their leaders? *(Six council members were chosen by the London Company back in England; their names were revealed on landing in Virginia. The council members elected a president to lead the colony.)*
3. Why was Jamestown a poor location for a settlement? *(swampy ground, bad water and climate, mosquitoes spread malaria)*

◉ Ponder
Why does it sound as if the early settlers in Jamestown were in great need of a good leader?

☑ Question Chart

DISCUSS

1. Distribute Resource 2 (TG page 77). What could this map have shown the settlers at Jamestown regarding a Northwest Passage? *(The map shows that the Appalachian Mountains would block any Northwest Passage connecting Virginia and the Pacific Ocean.)*
2. What effect did Spain's earlier interest in the area have on the English colonists at Jamestown? *(the Indians were hostile; English colonists feared an attack by the Spanish so they settled land they could defend but which was otherwise a bad choice)*
3. What were some of the problems the Jamestown colonists faced in their first months? *(incompetent leaders, fighting, men unprepared and unwilling to work, London Company policy, disease, starvation, hostile Indians)*

WRITE

Have students look at the picture on page 26 of Jamestown in 1607. Ask them to write an ad for an English newspaper, in which they encourage people to come join the settlers in Virginia.

L I T E R A C Y   L I N K S

Words to Discuss

malaria	incompetent
typhoid	dysentery

Have students use a dictionary as well as the context of Chapter 4 to determine the meanings of the words. Discuss: Which of these words are names of diseases? *(malaria, typhoid, dysentery)* What is the opposite of incompetent? *(competent)* What other prefixes, like in-, turn a word into its opposite? *(un-, a-, dis-, anti-)* Give a few examples.

Reading Skills
Understanding Primary Sources

Have students read the margin note on page 25. Ask the following questions. ANALYZING

- What mistake about Virginia geography did the London Company make? *(that there was a river leading to the Pacific Ocean)*
- What other features of the writing show that it is from another time? *(unusual capitalization; use of words like* runneth, amongst, bendeth, portable *for* navigable, *and* find out *for* build; *different spelling,* divers *for* diverse)
- Paraphrase the excerpt and break it into smaller, punctuated sentences. *(When you land on the coast of Virginia, build a safe fort at the entrance to a navigable river. If possible choose the river that comes from farthest inland. If you discover a river with two main branches, follow the one that bends toward the Northwest. It leads to the Pacific Ocean.)*

John Smith

Through tough, fair leadership and the ability to communicate and trade with the Indians, John Smith helped Jamestown survive its difficult early months.

ASK

1. What attracted John Smith to the 1607 trip to Virginia? *(He was an adventurer. He saw possibilities for the future in an English New World)*

2. What items did John Smith offer the Indians in trade? What did he get in return? *(Smith—shovels, axes, blankets; Indians—corn)*

3. Joy Hakim says that John Smith had "more than nine lives." Why does she say this? *(He survived many dangers: he was threatened by Indians; ambushed by Indians; stung by a stingray; burned by exploding gunpowder.)*

DISCUSS

1. Describe some of the ways John Smith helped his fellow colonists when he became the leader of Jamestown. *(He put colonists to work, traded with Powhatans for food, learned where Indians hunted and fished.)*

2. How did the Powhatans treat John Smith? *(They seemed undecided about him: they traded with him, respected him and adopted him into their tribe as an honorary chief; but they also threatened his life.)* Respond to Joy Hakim's question on page 30, "What would you have done if you were a Powhatan?"

3. Who was Pocahontas and how did she help the Jamestown colony? *(a princess, the Powhatan's favorite daughter; brought colonists food; may have saved John Smith's life when the Powhatan threatened him; warned Smith of an ambush)*

Ponder
John Smith's motto was, "If any would not work, neither should he eat." Why does this motto make sense for a new colony?

✔ **Question Chart**

WRITE

Ask students to write a brief sketch of John Smith, including the qualities and accomplishments that made him a good leader.

LITERACY LINKS

Words to Discuss

capital punishment
stingray
werowance

Have students use a dictionary as well as context to determine the meanings of the words. Discuss: What are some other meanings for the word *capital*? *("the seat of government"; "money")* Have students make a two-column chart titled *John Smith* with the headings *Achievements* and *Accidents*. In each column have students list appropriate details from the chapter, starting with two words from the list above.

Reading Skills
Identifying Point of View

Explain to students that they can discover what Joy Hakim thinks of John Smith from the words she uses to describe him. What are the adjectives and phrases used to characterize him? *(tough, no-nonsense, liked adventure, intelligent, curious, fair, honest, natural trader)* Does she have a positive or negative opinion of Smith? *(positive)* INFERRING

Skills Connection
Geography

Have students locate the Rappahannock and Roanoke rivers on the map on Resource 2 (TG page 77). Ask: In what states are these rivers found today? *(Roanoke flows through Virginia and North Carolina; Rappahannock is in Virginia.)*

The Starving Time

During the winter of 1609-1610, Jamestown was all but wiped out. Besieged by the Indians and unable to trade or hunt, the settlers ran out of food. Starvation shrank the settlement from 500 people in October 1609 to just 60 in May 1610.

ASK

1. When John Smith left for England in 1609, what made him think the colonists had enough food? *(The storehouses contained 10 weeks' worth of food; settlers had hens, chickens, goats, pigs; corn expected from Indians; game in woods and fish in rivers.)*

2. How did some settlers escape the Starving Time? *(They ran away and joined the Indians.)*

3. How did the Powhatan siege affect Jamestown settlers? *(The siege contributed to starvation among the settlers because they could not get past the Indians to hunt and fish.)*

⊚ Ponder
Would Powhatan have behaved differently if John Smith had been around?

✓ Question Chart

DISCUSS

1. Besides food supplies, what evidence is given in the chapter that the colony was prospering when John Smith left in October 1609? *(More colonists had arrived—a total of 500—including two women.)*

2. What are some possible reasons for the Starving Time? *(Drought, settlers refused to share with each other, the Powhatans refused to trade and laid siege to Jamestown.)*

3. How might a drought have affected the food supply of the colony? *(Crops were not as plentiful, Indians lacked supplies of corn, animals died.)*

WRITE

Have students imagine they are one of the settlers who left the stockade and went to join the Powhatans. Ask students to write a brief farewell note explaining why he or she is leaving Jamestown.

LITERACY LINKS

Words to Discuss

siege	stockade
drought	famished

Have students use a dictionary as well as context to determine the meanings of the words. Discuss: How do these words relate to the Starving Time? *(The siege and unequal distribution of food inside the stockade caused people to be famished; the drought affected the Indians' food supply.)*

Reading Skills
Using Primary and Secondary Sources

Draw students' attention to the two sections of italicized text on pages 32 and 33. Explain that both sections describe events in Jamestown. Have students read the two sections. Then ask: Which is a primary source and which is a secondary source? *(The poem is a secondary source—written much later by a poet who wasn't there; the other text is a primary source—*written by a participant.) What do the two sections add to the chapter? *(The poem gives a sense of the positive mood of the colonists before the Starving Time; the quote underlines the horror of the Starving Time.)* What line in the poem hints at trouble to come? *(next to last line, "and they had not long to live")* ANALYZING

THINKING ABOUT THE THEMES

The following questions will help students relate the book's themes to the content of Part 1. You may wish to use the questions for classroom discussion or have students answer them in written form.

1. Why did the London Company send English settlers to Virginia in 1607? How did their goals change after they arrived? *(The settlers came for gold and to find a Northwest Passage; when they found no gold and no passage, their goal became survival, which meant dealing with the Powhatans.)*

2. Who were the first settlers in Jamestown? *(They were all Englishmen, either gentlemen or yeomen.)* How did this lack of diversity affect the survival of the colony? *(Most lacked the skills necessary for surviving in Virginia.)*

3. What conflicts developed between the Powhatans and the colonists? *(The Powhatans attacked and killed colonists. They traded with John Smith but also were hostile to him. After he left the colony, they no longer gave food to the colonists. During the Starving Time they laid siege to Jamestown and kept the colonists from hunting and fishing.)*

4. Draw students' attention to the themes that have been posted around the room. Give them the opportunity to explore the relevance of these themes to Part 1. Accept choices that are supported by sound reasoning.

ASSESSING PART 1

Use Check-Up 1 (TG page 69) to assess student learning.

NOTE FROM JOY HAKIM

What we want is for children to have a sense of the journey through time. But for most children, memorized dates have little meaning. A sophisticated sense of time comes gradually. As far as expecting children to remember dates, I believe only a few key years are essential.

PROJECTS AND ACTIVITIES

▶ Powhatan Life in 1600—A Diorama

Have the class form groups, each group researching a different aspect of Powhatan life in 1600—housing, hunting, fishing, farming, children's play, the visit of a great chief. Have the groups come together to create and display a diorama based on their research.

▶ Jamestown Newspaper

Divide the class into four groups. Assign each group the job of creating an issue of a newspaper, *The Jamestown Journal*. The issues could be Spring 1607, Autumn 1607, Autumn 1609, and Spring 1610. Topics for articles could be colony leadership, work, food, John Smith, and relations with Powhatans. For more information check the Virtual Jamestown Website at *http://jefferson.village. virginia.edu/vcdh/jamestown/*.

▶ A Colonial Conversation

Have students work in trios, each playing the role of Powhatan, Pocahontas, or John Smith. What might these people have said to one another? Call for volunteers to present their dialogues to the class.

▶ WANTED: Another John Smith

Have students in small groups imagine they are colonists at Jamestown creating a want ad for a new leader like John Smith. The ads should show that students understand the qualities John Smith had that benefited the colony.

▶ Fact Sheet: The Thirteen English Colonies

Distribute Resource 3 (TG page 78) and complete as much of the Virginia section as possible. Have students keep the charts on hand to complete as they gather more information.

★★ **FACTS TO SHARE** ★★

Like other Indians, the Powhatans grew corn, squash, and beans in small mounds. They planted the three crops together for a reason. The tall corn stalks supported the beans. The squash vines provided a groundcover, which made weeding unnecessary. The beans fixed nitrogen in the soil, which kept the soil healthy.

INTRODUCING PART 2

The Seeds Take Root

Here's how John Smith described Jamestown's work program in 1608: "4 hours each day was spent in worke, the rest pastimes and merry exercise." To survive, the colonists had to change their ways and adapt to new realities. So did the Powhatans. Whenever the two cultures stopped trying to understand each other, a deadly conflict erupted.

SETTING GOALS

The goals for students in Part 2 are to:
- understand Jamestown's diversity.
- consider the pros and cons of growing tobacco in Virginia.
- trace the development of representative government in Virginia.
- compare and contrast English and Powhatan culture.
- describe the roles and importance of key colonists and Native Americans.

GETTING INTERESTED

1. To begin Part 2, inform students that they will learn how the Virginia colony survived and flourished. Have students preview Chapters 7-12 for clues about that survival and the price the colonists paid for success.

2. Help students understand the idea of cultures—how people develop a way of life based on where they live, what they believe, and their needs and desires. Point out that the English and Powhatans each had its own culture. Ask: which illustration shows a Powhatan adapting to English culture? *(Pocahontas on page 49)* Which illustrations show Powhatans and English in conflict? *(Powhatans attacking colonists on pages 45 and 49)*

⧗ Working with Timelines

Direct students' attention to the class timeline and tell them that Chapters 7-12 cover only twelve years in Jamestown, 1610 to 1622. Ask: Why are so many chapters devoted to Jamestown? Why is it so important? *(Possible response: If Jamestown hadn't survived, the English might have colonized somewhere else—or given up entirely; the records reveal a lot of information about the struggles of the early settlers.)*

🌐 Using Maps

To help students understand why colonists kept coming to America despite hardships, refer students to the map on pages 180-181. Have them contrast the landmass of eastern North America with the size of England. Ask: Why might English people want to come to America? *(England is very small; English people wanted land.)*

A Lord, A Hurricane, A Wedding

As the survivors of the Starving Time set sail for England, a fresh contingent of colonists arrived, giving the settlement new purpose. They left unhealthy Jamestown and built a settlement farther inland while developing better relations with the Powhatans.

ASK

1. Why did all the Jamestown colonists try to leave in the spring of 1610? Who made them stay? *(The newcomers were sick and those who had spent the winter in Jamestown were starving. Lord de la Warr, the new governor, made them stay.)*

2. How did Pocahontas come to live in Henrico? *(She was captured and held hostage.)*

3. Answer the question posed by Joy Hakim on page 35: "What state is named for Lord de la Warr?" *(Delaware)*

4. What happened to Pocahontas in England? *(She met King James; she was called Lady Rebecca and treated as a celebrity, she saw John Smith; she caught smallpox and died.)*

DISCUSS

1. What did Thomas Dale do for the colony? *(moved the settlement up the James River to Henrico, a healthier spot; made sure everyone worked; imposed rules)*

2. How did Pocahontas help to bring peace between Indians and colonists? *(She adapted to English ways and fell in love with John Rolfe. She changed her name to Rebecca and married Rolfe with the blessing of her Indian relatives)*

3. Pocahontas had three names: Matoax ("Little Snow Feather"), Pocahontas ("Playful"), and Rebecca (her English name). What do they reveal about her character? *(Each name stands for an aspect of her life: her Native American heritage, her cheerful disposition which led to her role as a go-between when Jamestown was first settled, and her ability to adapt to English ways and beliefs.)*

WRITE

Ask students to write a diary entry for Pocahontas. The entry should describe a significant time in her life (her capture, her feelings for John Rolfe, her trip to England).

Ponder
Would the Starving Time have happened if the English settlers who came to Jamestown in 1607 had been led by Sir Thomas Dale?

 **Question Chart**

L I T E R A C Y   L I N K S

Words to Discuss

> entangled   abound
> hostage

Have students use a dictionary and context to determine meanings. Discuss: Which word has a prefix? *(entangled)* Which word comes from the Latin word abundare, "to overflow"? *(abound)* What is another English word that comes from the same Latin word? *(abundance)* What famous hostage is discussed in Chapter 7? *(Pocahontas)*

Reading Skills
Evaluating Illustrations

Have students examine the portrait of Pocahontas on page 35. Ask these questions. INFERRING

- How did the artist present Pocahontas in the painting? *(as Lady Rebecca)*
- From the painting, what can you tell about Pocahontas's adaptation to England? *(From her clothing, you can assume that she adapted to England well.)*

- How would someone looking at the painting learn about Pocahontas's Powhatan roots? *(by reading the words around the picture)*
- How would you describe Pocahontas's expression? *(Responses will vary.)*

A Share in America

In search of adventure, riches, or escape, 10,000 English settlers made their way to Virginia. Only 2,000 survived. The others failed to accommodate to their new surroundings, were killed by Indians, or died from starvation and disease.

ASK

1. What were some reasons English people continued to come to Virginia after the Starving Time? *(to find gold, for adventure, for a better life; some were criminals and unwanted in England)*

2. Some people in England had "fine ideas" about life in America? What were those ideas? *(Native Americans and colonists could live side by side and learn from each other; America was an ideal place where everyone was happy.)*

3. Why did Europeans invest in the Virginia Company? *(to profit from gold, to save Indians from the Spaniards, to take part in a national venture)*

4. Why did Indians think English colonists were savages? *(They didn't bathe so they smelled; they didn't know how to hunt or to dress in the hot climate.)*

🌀 Ponder

Refer students to the last two lines of the poem about Virginia on page 37: "We hope to plant a nation/Where none before hath stood." What do these lines say about the poet's attitude toward the Powhatan empire?

✔ Question Chart

DISCUSS

1. What incidents show that the relationship between colonists and Indians was worsening? *(William Tucker poisoned 200 Indians; other colonists burned Indian villages in revenge for the Starving Time.)*

2. Why do you think Joy Hakim says, "If you ever go to a strange land, try to see how the natives live"? *(Many colonists died because they didn't learn how the Powhatans hunted, fished, raised crops, or gathered food.)*

3. In "Class System," the margin note on page 38, Joy Hakim says: "the idea that gentlemen should not work will be rejected in the New World." What does she mean? *(Life in Virginia was hard; no one could survive without working. Conditions in the colonies would not encourage the class system that was in place in England.)*

WRITE

Have partners write a dialogue between a young Jamestown colonist and a friend in England. The settler should try to convince the friend to come to America, while the friend argues for remaining in England.

LITERACY LINKS

Words to Discuss

tidewater	promoter
aristocracy	share

Have students use a dictionary and context to determine meanings. Discuss: Which words apply to both England and Virginia? *(aristocracy, promoter, share)* Which word applies to the Virginia colony? *(tidewater)* Which word has the suffix meaning "government or rule," from the Greek word for power? *(aristocracy)*

Reading Skills
Evaluating Word Choice

Direct students' attention to the last three paragraphs on page 39. Ask a volunteer to read the text aloud. Then give the following instructions.
ANALYZING

• Pick out the adjectives that convey the author's message that it wasn't easy to "be an Englishman in the wilderness." *(60-pound, metal, wool, blistered, biting, crazy, angry, swampy, heavy, loud, unhealthy, clanking, scared off)*

• Give examples of verbs in these paragraphs that put readers back in the 1600s in Virginia. *(picture, imagine, look, remember)*

• What words are contrasted with loud, clanking armor? *(quiet as falling leaves)* Why does the author do this? *(to make the point that Indians knew how to hunt deer in the woods and the English did not)*

Jamestown Makes It

The Virginia colonists never found riches in gold. Instead, riches came to them in the form of tobacco. The need for labor to work the tobacco fields brought indentured servants and African slaves to Virginia.

ASK

1. From the English colonists' point of view, what was the problem with tobacco as a crop? *(It required hard work in the fields.)*
2. Why didn't indentured servants want to come to Virginia? *(so many colonists had died there)*
3. Who were the first Africans brought to Virginia? *(indentured servants who became free after a certain period of time)*

DISCUSS

1. Why does Joy Hakim equate tobacco with gold? *(because tobacco was a profitable crop that made people's fortunes in Virginia)*
2. What did King James think of tobacco? What industry did he want to start in Virginia to replace it? *(He hated tobacco and wanted to start a silk industry instead.)*
3. How did slavery start in Virginia? *(Africans were first brought as indentured servants; tobacco planters enslaved them to avoid having to pay for new servants every few years.)*
4. It often was easier for Indians than for black people to run away when they were enslaved. Why was this so? *(Indians, native to America, were very familiar with the countryside; the surroundings were new and strange to black people.)*

⊚ Ponder
Slavery in America started "without much thought, which is the way bad things often happen." Can you think of other examples where that statement would be true?

✓ Question Chart

WRITE

Have students prepare a proclamation that could have been issued by King James, in which he advises people not to use tobacco.

L I T E R A C Y   L I N K S

Words to Discuss

enslaved   tobacco
indentured

Have students use a dictionary and context to determine meanings. Discuss: Which English word was originally a Taino Indian word? *(tobacco)* Have students make a chart with two columns headed *indentured* and *enslaved*. Ask them to add descriptions of what it meant to be *indentured* or *enslaved*.

Reading Skills
Understanding Text Organization
Discuss that nonfiction often has a cause-and-effect organization. A cause may have several effects. Also, an effect often causes another effect (a causal chain). For example, the colonists' poor planning and the Powhatans' siege of Jamestown caused the Starving Time, which caused the colonists to take revenge on the Powhatans. Ask partners to make a cause-and-effect

flowchart of Chapter 9, starting with *The English wanted to get rich in Virginia* and ending with *Settlers enslaved Africans.* *(Other items might include: John Rolfe developed a popular type of tobacco; tobacco farming required field workers; indentured servants were brought in from Europe and Africa; planters didn't want to lose indentured servants after a certain time.)* CONNECTING

1619—A Big Year

In 1619, certain events in Virginia profoundly affected the course of American history: the arrival of Englishwomen clinched English permanence; the introduction of African workers foreshadowed almost 250 years of slavery; and the introduction of representative government foreshadowed self-government.

ASK

1. What event of 1619 showed that the English were in America to stay? *(The arrival of a boatload of women showed that the English settlers wanted to marry and have children.)*

2. From what countries in Europe besides England did Virginia colonists come? *(Poland, Holland or the Netherlands, Germany, Italy)*

3. Why did Polish workers go on strike in 1619? *(English men and women had more rights and freedoms than people in other European nations at the time.)*

4. What was the first representative government of Englishmen in America? *(Virginia House of Burgesses)*

◎ Ponder
Why was it smart for the Virginia Company in 1619 to let settlers have land of their own?

✔ Question Chart

DISCUSS

1. What were the five "firsts" that occurred in 1619, and what were their effects? *(first boatload of Africans—paved the way for slavery; first boatload of women—made Virginia a permanent colony; first labor strike—established that settlers from other countries had the same rights as English settlers; first time English settlers could own land—gave them a reason to work hard; first representative government—beginning of self-government in American colonies)*

2. What was the result of English colonies having "open doors"? *(People came from other countries to settle in English colonies.)*

3. Which two examples in Chapter 10 tell how valuable tobacco had become? *(tobacco was used to pay a fine; wife cost 120 pounds of tobacco. In both cases, we see that tobacco was used as money.)*

WRITE

Have partners imagine they are reporters covering the arrival of the boatload of women in 1619. Have them write questions to ask one of the women—as well as her responses.

LITERACY LINKS

Words to Discuss

strike veto
pluralistic tax

Have students use a dictionary and context to determine meanings. Discuss: Which words refer to changes or events in Jamestown after 1619? *(all of them)* Which word comes from a Latin verb meaning "I forbid"? *(veto)* Have students make a word web for *pluralistic,* using related words from the chapter.

Reading Skills
Evaluating Text

Read the margin note on page 42 aloud. Ask: PREDICTING

• What is the meaning of "They won't want to give up that power"? *(The Burgesses will want to keep the power to collect taxes.)*

• Who might want to take that power away? *(the royal governor, the King)*

• What may happen between the Burgesses and the governor? *(There will be conflict over the taxes.)*

Meeting Individual Needs
Visual Learners

Have students make index cards for each of the "firsts" of 1619—women, Africans, labor strike, elected lawmakers, chance to own land. On each card, have them note relevant information from the chapter. They can color-code the topics and cards.

Indians vs. Colonists

Whether the Europeans and the Indians started out with the best intentions or the worst, bloody conflict was inevitable. The Europeans wanted more and more land, and the Indians knew the loss of their land would destroy their way of life.

ASK

1. How did colonists "use up" land? *(They cut trees in forests; people settled on land.)*

2. Why were uncut forests important to the Indians? *(They hunted wild animals that lived in the woods; when the woods were gone, there were no animals to hunt.)*

3. How did Pennsylvania colonists cheat the Delaware chief, Lappawinsoe? *(They ran over "as much land as they could cover in a day and a half.")*

DISCUSS

1. According to Joy Hakim, what was the main reason Indians and colonists had no hope of living in peace? *(Colonists wanted land the Indians used.)*

2. Why do you think neither side would compromise? *(Both Indians and colonists felt their existence was at stake.)*

3. Consider the cartoon on page 45 and answer the question posed in the caption. *(Students should understand that in interactions between Indians and colonists, kindness was not always met with kindness.)*

4. The author states that arrogance (thinking you are better than others) was a problem. What examples does she give to back up her statement? *(Aztecs who believed that anyone who wasn't Aztec was inferior; people who think their religion is better than anyone else's)*

⊙ Ponder

The Virginia governor said (page 45): "Either we must clear the Indians out of the country, or they must clear us out." How could Indians and colonists have shared the land?

✓ Question Chart

WRITE

Ask students to write a diary entry that a young Native American may have written in the 1620s. They are to suppose that settlers have recently arrived in their region. What are their impressions? their fears? their confusion? their hopes?

LITERACY LINKS

Words to Discuss

arrogance   engraving
bigot   swindle

Have students use a dictionary and context to determine meanings. Discuss: Which words relate to the colonist-Indian relationship? *(arrogance, bigot, swindle)* What do those words say about the relationship? Which word names the process that brought art to people who couldn't afford paintings? *(engraving)*

Reading Skills
Evaluating Information

On page 46, have students read the margin note and the caption under the upper illustration. Then ask them to look at the engraving *William Penn's Treaty.* Explain that the text and illustration tell about the relationship between colonists and Indians. Ask these questions: ANALYZING

• What evidence of what Lawton calls the colonists' "moral deformities and evils" is in the illustration or caption? *(The caption describes how colonists cheated Indians.)*

• In the engraving, is the mood peaceful or tense? *(peaceful)* What do the man's out-flung arms *(center)* indicate? *(welcome, acceptance)*

• Which more accurately shows the colonist-Indian relationship: the engraving or Lawton's "Field of Blood" comment? *(Lawton's comment)*

Massacre in Virginia, Poverty in England

Colonist-Indian antagonism flared into massive violence. Yet immigration from England continued because crippling troubles there kept pushing people to leave. At the same time, slavery was becoming more deeply rooted in Virginia.

ASK

1. Who spread the word about the 1622 massacre and saved the lives of some Jamestown colonists? *(a Powhatan named Chanco)*
2. What was King James's response to the massacre? *(He made Virginia a royal colony and closed the Virginia Company.)*
3. What happened to Virginia Company stockholders when King James made Virginia a royal colony? *(They lost the money they had invested.)*
4. For how long had slavery existed? *(from back in biblical times)* How did Europeans get started in the slave trade? *(In 1442, the Portuguese were looking for ways to make money, and started selling captured Africans as slaves.)*

⊚ Ponder
Irony is the use of words that seem to express the opposite of what you really mean. In what way is the title of the feature on page 50—America, Land of the Free—ironic?

✔ Question Chart

DISCUSS

1. What is a possible reason for the massacre of 1622? *(Opechancanough, Pocahontas's uncle, decided to get rid of the colonists who he felt were stealing the Indians' land.)*
2. Why did English people continue to come to Virginia after the massacre of 1622? *(The population of England was growing; there were few jobs; farmers were being forced off the land; London was full of beggars and starving people; they wanted a better life.)*
3. What kind of a king was King James? *(He was thoughtful and well-read but not a strong political leader.)*

WRITE

Have students complete Resource 5 (TG page 80). Then ask them to suppose they are in Jamestown writing to a friend in London. In the letter they should refer to the leaflet, explaining why it's helpful to someone planning a move to Jamestown.

LITERACY LINKS

Words to Discuss

sachem
divine right

Have students use a dictionary and context to determine meanings. Discuss: What is a connection between these words? *(Each word refers to a leader: a sachem was an Indian leader; divine right was claimed by European monarchs.)*

Reading Skills
Identifying Visual Clues

Have students look at the picture on page 49. Ask: What does this picture show? *(the Great Massacre of 1622)* Is the event shown from the English or Indian point of view? *(English)* How do you know? *(only English settlers are being killed)* What might new colonists think about Indians from this picture? *(Indians are to be feared.)* INFERRING

Skills Connection
Geography

Display a world map. Have students locate Portugal and Ghana. Ask students to trace possible sea routes that the Portuguese could have taken to West Africa. Then have them use the map scale to figure out roughly how many miles the Portuguese traveled to reach Ghana.

THINKING ABOUT THE THEMES

The following questions will help students relate the book's themes to the content of Part 2. You may wish to use the questions for classroom discussion or have students answer them in written form.

1. What changes were required of English settlers when they came to Virginia? *(To survive, even gentlemen had to work hard and learn new ways of hunting and farming.)*

2. In what ways were the lives of the Powhatans changed by the English? *(They suffered diseases and loss of their land; their villages were attacked; their existence was threatened.)*

3. What evidence of diversity was there among the settlers in Virginia after 1610? *(There were people from other parts of Europe, poor people and convicts, indentured servants, yeomen and gentlemen, enslaved Africans.)*

4. Draw students' attention to the themes that have been posted around the room. Give them the opportunity to explore the relevance of these themes to Part 2. Accept choices that are supported by sound reasoning.

ASSESSING PART 2

Use Check-Up 2 (TG page 70) to assess student learning.

NOTE FROM JOY HAKIM

How do you teach about right and wrong? Through stories—the stories of heroes, heroines, and villains. You may get away with misbehavior in the long run, but hardly anyone escapes the judgment of history.

PROJECTS AND ACTIVITIES

▶ Who Said It?

Distribute Resource 4 (TG page 79) and have students complete it and discuss their answers.

▶ Reporting on Jamestown

Write the following headlines on the chalkboard: *Welcome to Jamestown, Ladies; Glassmakers Strike for Rights; Tobacco Takes Root, Laws for Virginia Made in Virginia; Whose Land Is It?* Have students work in groups to collect facts for a story to match each headline. To organize their facts, have students divide a sheet of paper into sections labeled *Who? What? When? Where? Why?*

▶ Model of a Storm at Sea

Have a small group of students make a wave bottle to demonstrate to the class. They can use an empty, clear plastic, 2-liter bottle with cap. Prepare a mixture of equal parts mineral oil and tap water and add it to the bottle through a funnel. (Do not taste the mixture.) Have students put in several drops of blue food coloring and add a plastic object (to represent a ship at sea). Seal tightly and pass the bottle around, shaking and rocking it to make "waves." Ask students to observe what happens to the plastic object in the waves. Then have them imagine they survived a storm at sea and write a diary entry about it.

▶ What to Bring

Distribute Resource 5 (TG page 80). Have pairs of students read it and answer the questions. Discuss answers with the whole class.

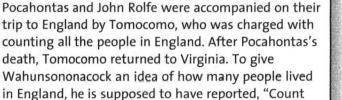

★ ★ FACTS TO SHARE ★ ★

Pocahontas and John Rolfe were accompanied on their trip to England by Tomocomo, who was charged with counting all the people in England. After Pocahontas's death, Tomocomo returned to Virginia. To give Wahunsononacock an idea of how many people lived in England, he is supposed to have reported, "Count the stars in the sky, and leaves on the trees, and the sand upon the seashore."

Colonizing Massachusetts

William Bradford, chronicler of the Pilgrims' experience at Plymouth, described their thoughts on reaching North America: "What could now sustain them but the spirit of God and His Grace?" It was their powerful religious feelings that had brought them to a new colony, and it was their faith—and plenty of help from Native Americans—that would sustain the Pilgrims through the trials they faced.

SETTING GOALS

The goals for students in Part 3 are to:
- evaluate the relationship between the Wampanoag and the Pilgrims.
- compare and contrast the Pilgrims and Puritans.
- understand the Puritans' views of other religions and education.
- describe a typical New England town during colonial times.

GETTING INTERESTED

1. Have students preview Chapters 13-16 by scanning the chapter titles, illustrations, headings, and margin notes. Ask: How do you think colonizing Massachusetts in 1620 was different from colonizing Jamestown in 1607? *(Massachusetts colonists could learn from the mistakes made at Jamestown.)*

2. Write the word *motive* on the board. Explain that a motive is a feeling or a need that causes a person to act a certain way. Ask: what motives brought colonists to Jamestown? *(to find gold; to make money for investors, for adventure, land, a new life; because they were kidnapped and forced to go)* Elicit who were the first settlers to come to New England and why. *(the Pilgrims, who came in search of a home where they could practice their religion in peace)*

 Working with Timelines
Ask students to turn to the Chronology of Events on page 170 to find out when the settlement of New England began. *(1620)* Ask: How long was this after the first settlers reached Jamestown? *(13 years)* When did the Pilgrims establish peace with the Wampanoag? *(1621)* When did the Great Massacre in Virginia take place? *(1622)*

 Using Maps
Distribute Resource 6 (TG page 81) and have students compare the maps. (Map 1 shows many Indian groups all over New England and few European settlements. Map 2 shows the Indians restricted to Maine and New Hampshire and many more European settlements.) Based on what happened in Virginia, have students predict why this change occurred in New England. *(After a conflict with the Indians, colonists will take Indian land.)*

The Mayflower: Saints and Strangers

In England, a group of people who were dissatisfied with the established church wanted to separate themselves from it. Known first as Separatists and then as Pilgrims, they fled first to Holland, and then in 1620 went to America.

ASK

1. How can you tell the Separatists were devoted to their beliefs? *(They were willing to leave their homes and go to Holland for religious freedom.)*

2. Why did the Pilgrims leave Holland? *(They wanted their children to grow up English, not Dutch.)*

3. Who were the Strangers? *(People who traveled with the Pilgrims to North America but who left England for adventure or a better life, not for religious reasons.)*

4. What did John Smith offer to do for the Pilgrims? *(He offered to be their guide; instead they used his guidebook to New England since it was cheaper than hiring him.)*

⊚ Ponder
What do you think the king of England thought about the Mayflower Compact?

✓ Question Chart

DISCUSS

1. Why was there religious dissension in England in the 1600s? *(Anglicans and Catholics were hostile to each other; Puritans and Separatists wanted to change the established Anglican Church; all were intolerant of religious views other than their own.)*

2. Why was the Mayflower Compact a significant document in our nation's history? *(It established self-government in a new colony.)*

3. What evidence can you give that the place the Pilgrims called Plymouth was not a wilderness? *(A 1605 map shows an Indian village located there; they found fields cleared for planting.)*

WRITE

Have students suppose they are John Smith. Referring to "their" accomplishments in Virginia, they should write letters to the Pilgrims, offering their services as guides.

L I T E R A C Y   L I N K S

Words to Discuss

| Separatists | Puritans |
| Strangers | Pilgrims |

Discuss: Which two words describe the same people? *(Separatists, Pilgrims)* Which word describes people who traveled with the Pilgrims to New England? *(Strangers)* Why are Puritans and Pilgrims often confused? *(Both groups objected to Anglican Church; both came to settle in New England.)* Which words are linked to the Mayflower? *(all except Puritans)*

Reading Skills
Using a Primary Source

Sourcebook: Read the Mayflower Compact (Source #4) aloud to the class. Then write this excerpt on the chalkboard: "We . . . covenant & combine ourselves together into a civil body politick . . . to enact, constitute, and frame such just & equal laws, ordinances, acts, constitutions, and offices . . . for the general good of the colony." Ask the following questions to help students better understand the Mayflower Compact. ANALYZING

- What is a "civil body politick"? *(a group of people who agree to work together to make laws)*

- What was meant by "general good of the colony"? *(anything that helped the people of the colony as a whole rather than benefiting one or more individuals)*

Pilgrims, Indians, and Puritans

Having arrived too late to plant crops, the Pilgrims struggled through their first year with the help of the Wampanoag. Meanwhile, times grew harder in England for another group of dissenters—the Puritans.

ASK

1. Who were three Indians whose friendship helped the Pilgrims? *(Samoset, Squanto, Massasoit)*

2. Who provided most of the food at the harvest festival in 1621? *(Massasoit and his people, who also brought five deer)*

3. How did the Pilgrims help Massasoit? *(Edward Winslow made a nourishing broth that helped him recover from an illness.)*

Ponder
What significance does the Thanksgiving holiday have for you?

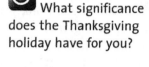 **Question Chart**

DISCUSS

1. In what ways did Massasoit and Squanto save the Pilgrims? *(They agreed to a peace treaty; provided food; taught them how to fish and farm so they wouldn't starve.)*

2. Distribute Resource 7 (TG page 82). Have students answer the questions and discuss their answers.

3. Why did the Puritans make plans to come to North America? *(King James persecuted the Puritans because they wanted to change ("purify") the Church of England; they disagreed with his economic policies.)*

WRITE

Have students, as Pilgrims in 1621, write a note to Squanto and Massasoit, thanking them for their help.

LITERACY LINKS

Words to Discuss

frugal	kidnap
treaty	moderate
succotash	purify
harvest	

Have students use a dictionary and context to determine the meanings of the words. Which words apply to Puritans? *(moderate, purify)* Which words apply to the Pilgrims? *(frugal, harvest, treaty)* Which apply to the Wampanoags? *(succotash, treaty)*

Reading Skills
Evaluating Visuals

Have students study the illustration on page 58 and then answer the following questions. CONNECTING

- How does the scene continue the myth that the Pilgrims provided food to the Indians instead of the other way around? *(A Pilgrim woman carries a serving dish to Indians, most of the food is on serving dishes; women are bringing food out of a Pilgrim home; foods introduced to the Pilgrims by the Wampanoag seem to belong to the Pilgrims.)*

- There were almost twice as many Indians as Pilgrims at the actual feast in 1621. Is that what's shown in the illustration? *(No, Indians are outnumbered by Pilgrims.)*

Meeting Individual Needs
Reteaching

English language learners may have difficulty pronouncing Indian names and words in this chapter. Add Indian names to the pronunciation chart students created in Part 1.

Puritans, Puritans, and More Puritans

In 1630, Puritans arrived in New England and settled the Massachusetts Bay Colony. They set up a government that gave them the right to follow their own religious principles— but they did not tolerate any other religion.

ASK

1. Why did Puritans come to New England? *(to practice their religion in peace; to live by the rules of the Bible)* How many came between 1630 and 1640? *(20,000)*

2. How did the Puritans feel about other religions? *(They were intolerant. They persecuted those different from themselves.)*

3. What Quaker belief did the Puritans particularly dislike? *(that ministers aren't necessary, and people are able to find God on their own)*

@ **Ponder**
Would you like to live in a country without laws? What would the country be like?

DISCUSS

1. Why was a charter important for a colony? *(Charters spelled out the rules about running the colony. A charter allowed members of a colony to govern themselves.)*

2. In what way was the General Court a type of democracy? *(Once a year church members got together to elect a governor and council.)* How democratic was it? *(Not all people could vote; only males could vote)*

3. Explain why the Massachusetts Bay Colony might have seemed like a theocracy but was not. *(The ministers were the most important people in the colony; however, they were not allowed to govern, so it was not a theocracy.)*

✔ **Question Chart**

WRITE

Ask students to work in small groups to write a first draft of a charter for the class. The charter should include rules of behavior and procedures for making decisions and settling disputes. Discuss the group drafts, combining elements of each for a final version.

LITERACY LINKS

Words to Discuss

autocracy   theocracy
democracy   aristocracy

Have students use a dictionary and context to determine the meanings of the words. Have students make a chart showing the Greek origins of these words: *auto* ("self"), *demos* ("people"), *theo* ("god"), and *aristos* ("best") combine with *kratos* ("power") to form the words.

Reading Skills
Understanding Rhetorical Devices

Starting with the fourth paragraph on page 60, read aloud through the first line on page 61. Ask the following questions to help students identify and understand the rhetorical device the author uses here. ANALYZING

• What does the author ask the reader to do in this section? *(pretend to be a Puritan)*

• How does she help the reader do this? *(She speaks to the reader as "you"; she tells the reader what to think as a Puritan.)*

• When Joy Hakim says "you've left your home and everything you know and love" and "You've crossed a fierce ocean to live as you wish," what does she want you to do, and why? *(to put yourself in the Puritans' place; to understand what the Puritans went through)*

Of Towns and Schools and Sermons

New England villages were well laid out and compact, with places for living, working, and meeting. Puritan laws regulated behavior, encouraged education, and fostered a strong religious ethic.

ASK

1. What problem did Puritan livestock create for the Indians? How was it solved? *(The Puritans' cattle, sheep and other grazing animals ate Indian crops; Puritans built fences around Indian fields and paid for damages.)*
2. What was the first book printed in the American colonies? *(the Bay Psalm Book)*
3. Why did the Puritans care so passionately about schooling? *(They wanted everyone to be able to read the Bible.)*

◎ **Ponder**
Joy Hakim says: "It isn't fun to be ignorant." Think of all the ways in which that statement is true!

☑ **Question Chart**

DISCUSS

1. How do we know the Puritans cared about schooling? *(They established Harvard College; passed laws requiring parents to teach children to read; required towns to hire teachers.)*
2. Explain how the Puritans tapped waterpower. *(Water from a river or stream turned a wheel that created power for a mill to grind wheat or saw wood.)*
3. Why might a Puritan boy or girl look forward to a daylong church service? *(There were no other forms of entertainment and only a few books.)*

WRITE

Have students suppose they are young settlers in the New England village illustrated on page 66. Ask them to write a letter to a friend back in England. Their letters should answer questions such as the following: What is it like to live in New England? What does one do during the week, and on Sundays? What is the function of a meetinghouse?

L I T E R A C Y   L I N K S

Words to Discuss

scold	stocks
common	blue law

Have students use a dictionary and context to determine the meanings of the words. Have students write each of these words in the center circle of a word web. Ask them to complete the webs with details from the text.

Reading Skills
Reading Primary Sources

Sourcebook: Read aloud the introduction to the Massachusetts School Laws (Source #5). Then have partners answer the following questions. CONNECTING

- What is the main idea of each law? *(1642—Parents and masters are responsible for their children's learning and religion; 1647—every township of 50 householders has to provide public education; towns of 100 householders have to provide a public school.)*
- Why are these important laws? *(They are the beginning of U. S. public education; they show that Puritans cared about education.)*

Skills Connection
Geography

Have students turn to the Resource map on page 185. What did the Native Americans in New England hunt? *(deer, elk, beaver)* What else did the land provide for its people? *(iron, timber, farmland)*

THINKING ABOUT THE THEMES

The following questions will help students relate the book's themes to the content of Part 3. You may wish to use the questions for classroom discussion or have students answer them in written form.

1. How did life change for the Wampanoags when the Pilgrims landed at Plymouth? *(They agreed to a peace treaty; there now were people inhabiting the village wiped out by disease.)*

2. Do you see a chance for conflict in the Massachusetts Bay Colony? Explain. *(It's likely that there will be conflict between Puritans and people of other beliefs; between Indians and Puritans.)*

3. How did the Puritans' beliefs about religion go along with ideas of diversity? *(Not very well; they believed that their religion was the only true one.)*

4. Draw students' attention to the themes that have been posted around the room. Give them the opportunity to explore the relevance of these themes to Part 3. Accept choices that are supported by sound reasoning.

ASSESSING PART 2

Use Check-Up 3 (TG page 71) to assess student learning.

NOTE FROM JOY HAKIM

I want your children to learn words from this book, and to learn to love words, too. I'd like them to become word detectives and go off sleuthing in the word-derivation forest.

PROJECTS AND ACTIVITIES

▶ Aboard the *Mayflower*

Use masking tape to mark a 7-foot by 2.5-foot area on the classroom floor. Note that this was the area assigned to one adult on board the *Mayflower*. Children got even less space. Have students take turns standing and moving in the space. Discuss how it feels to be in a cramped space for a long period of time. Ask: why were people willing to endure this hardship? *(a strong desire for religious freedom or adventure)* For more information about the Pilgrims, visit the Pilgrims Hall Museum Website at **www.pilgrimhall.org.**

▶ Write a Dialogue

Have students work in pairs to create a dialogue between Squanto and a Pilgrim. Remind students that Squanto speaks English and has been to England as a slave. An English sea captain returned him to North America. Ask students to answer the following questions as they write the dialogue: What, if anything, will Squanto tell the Pilgrim about his life? Will he reveal that he used to live where Plymouth is being built? His village was wiped out by disease; perhaps it's a painful subject. What will Squanto learn in this dialogue? What does the Pilgrim think when he or she hears Squanto speaking English as Samoset did? What will the Pilgrim learn in this dialogue? Have students present their dialogues to the class.

▶ Make a Decision

Have students imagine they are Puritans living in Massachusetts Bay Colony. Would they be willing to welcome people of other religions who want to come to the colony? Or do they want Massachusetts to be all-Puritan forever? Ask students to consider the benefits and drawbacks of both decisions.

★★ FACTS TO SHARE ★★

Squanto was taken to England by an English captain. He learned English and eventually returned to North America. He was again captured and enslaved in 1614, this time by a Spaniard. Squanto escaped from Spain, made his way to England, and was returned to Cape Cod. But he found his village deserted. The people there had died of a fast-spreading disease brought by European fishermen. In 1620 his empty village became Plymouth.

Growing Discontent in New England

Puritan Massachusetts was established as a model colony. "The eyes of all people are upon us," Governor Winthrop said. But diversity of opinions within the colony led to bitter conflict. The arrival of more Puritans and their desire for land led to violent conflict with Native Americans.

SETTING GOALS

The goals for students in Part 4 are to:
- understand conflicts between Puritans and Quakers.
- summarize events that led up to the witch trials in Salem.
- compare and contrast Native American and European ideas about land use and land ownership.
- understand the significance of the Wampanoag chief Metacom and the Pueblo leader Popé.

GETTING INTERESTED

1. Have students preview Chapters 17-23 by scanning titles, headings, illustrations, captions, margin notes, and quotations. Ask: Who are some of the people in the illustrations? What events are shown? *(Roger Williams, a Salem witch trial, Cotton Mather, King Philip, Priests and Indians, Don Diego de Vargas, the hanging of Mary Dyer)*

2. Help students identify a common thread among the illustrations. Most of the people or scenes they identified illustrate a conflict found in Part 4—individuals in conflict with Puritan authorities; Indians in conflict with colonists; common sense in conflict with witchcraft.

Working with Timelines
Tell students that Part 4 covers the years 1636-1680. Have them refer to the Chronology of Events on page 170 to find dates to add to their individual timelines. Remind them to take notes of important dates as they read and add them to the timeline after each chapter.

Using Maps
Have students turn to the map on age 82. Ask: What is this region called? *(New England)* Draw students' attention to the map of New Netherland on page 83. Make sure they understand it includes the same area shown on page 82. Ask: Why would maps of the same area be called by different names? *(European powers made maps to confirm their claims in North America.)* Ask students to infer why the area is called New England. *(because it was settled by the English)*

Roger Williams

Though a Puritan minister, Roger Williams held a number of distinctly non-Puritan ideas, many of which would later become central to American life. Banished from Massachusetts, he started a colony where others with unpopular beliefs found a home.

ASK

1. What was Roger Williams's profession? *(Puritan minister)*
2. What did Roger Williams preach about Indian lands? *(that they should not be taken from Indians)*
3. Why did Roger Williams leave Massachusetts Bay Colony, and what did he do next? *(To avoid being sent to England as punishment for his beliefs, he ran away from Puritan authorities, bought land from Indians, and founded a new colony.)*

DISCUSS

1. Which beliefs of Roger Williams's were unpopular with other Puritans? *(No one should be forced to believe in a religion; only taxes from church members should go to the church; people's beliefs should be respected; New England belonged to the Indians.)*
2. What does "freedom of conscience" mean and why is it an important right? *(People can choose a religion for themselves; religious belief is freely chosen.)*
3. **Sourcebook:** Read aloud from Source #6: "There goes many a ship to sea . . . seamen and all the passengers." Ask: why is a ship a good way to describe society? *(People on a ship have the same destination; they have to learn to cooperate with one another.)*

Ponder

Joy Hakim writes: "You can make people do things, but you can't make them believe what they don't want to believe." How have you found that statement to be true in your own life?

 **Question Chart**

WRITE

Have students suppose that it is the 17ᵗʰ century, and they are about to leave England for North America. In a letter to Roger Williams, they are to explain why they want to join his community in Rhode Island.

L I T E R A C Y   L I N K S

Words to Discuss

atheist
tenet
religious liberty
separation of church and state

Have students use a dictionary and the context of the chapter to determine the meanings of the words. Have individual students pick a word or phrase and explain how it relates it to Roger Williams. (atheists *came to Rhode Island*; two of his tenets *were* religious liberty *and* separation of church and state)

Reading Skills
Identifying Text Organization
On page 68, read aloud paragraphs 2-4. Ask the following questions.
ANALYZING

- What is the purpose of paragraph 2? *(to show similarities between Roger Williams and other Puritans)*
- How does the author let you know she is switching from similarities to differences? *(paragraph 3: But that's where "like the others" stops.)*
- What information do you expect to find in paragraph 4? *(differences between Roger Williams and other Puritans)*

Skills Connection
Geography

Have students locate Providence, Rhode Island on Resource 2 (TG page 77). Have them use the map scale to estimate how far Roger Williams had to travel from Boston to Providence. *(approximately 50 miles)* Discuss what the trip was like for a sick man in winter.

"Woman, Hold Your Tongue"

Like Roger Williams, Anne Hutchinson openly disagreed with certain Puritan beliefs and was banished for her outspokenness.

ASK

1. What did Anne Hutchinson do? *(She questioned the Puritan ministers' beliefs and shared her ideas with others.)*
2. Why did people listen to Anne Hutchinson? *(She was smart and they thought what she said about the Bible made sense.)*
3. Why was that a problem? *(Women were not supposed to speak out; no one was supposed to question the Puritan ministers.)*
4. What happened to Anne Hutchinson? *(She was put on trial and forced to leave Massachusetts. She traveled to Rhode Island and then to New York, where she was killed by Indians.)*

◉ Ponder
Anne Hutchinson accepted banishment rather than give up thinking for herself. What kind of person does that?

✓ Question Chart

DISCUSS

1. Why were Puritan leaders in Massachusetts so threatened by Anne Hutchinson? *(She was critical of them, and people listened to her. In their view, she did not behave the way a woman should.)*
2. Why do you think Anne Hutchinson went to Rhode Island when she left Massachusetts? *(Roger Williams had established a colony where people of different faiths were welcome.)*

WRITE

Draw students' attention to the description of *chattel* at the top of page 72. Have them write a paragraph comparing the rights of married American women then and now.

L I T E R A C Y   L I N K S

Words to Discuss

chattel   imprisoned
banished

On the chalkboard, make a three-column chart labeled *Anne Hutchinson, Catherine Marbury Scott,* and *Alice Tilley.* Have students put vocabulary words in each column that fit each woman, and explain why. (chattel—*all, married women were "property"*; banished—*Hutchinson, sent away*; imprisoned—*Tilley for medical malpractice, Scott for protesting treatment of Quakers*)

Reading Skills
Understanding a Primary Source

Have students read the Massachusetts Court Record on page 73. Discuss Hutchinson's trial, using these questions. INFERRING

- What happened at the trial? *(The court voted to banish Hutchinson.)*
- Who voted against banishment? *(Mr. Coddington, Mr. Colburn)*
- Who did not vote either way? *(Mr. Jennings)*

Have students look at the last exchange between Hutchinson and Governor Winthrop. Ask:

- What does Hutchinson ask the Court? *(Why am I being banished?)*
- What is Winthrop's answer? *(The Court knows why.)*

Why do you think the Governor refused to explain the Court's reasons to her? *(Because she was "chattel"; the Court didn't want to argue with her because she was an effective speaker.)*

Statues on the Common

Mary Dyer and other Quakers were persecuted by Puritans. Some were whipped, some were banished, and others were hanged. Their refusal to give in to oppression resulted in a change in Puritan laws.

ASK

1. Who was Mary Dyer? *(Mary Dyer was a Puritan who became a Quaker and returned to Massachusetts Bay Colony.)*
2. What did the Society of Friends (Quakers) believe about swearing allegiance to the king? *(They would not swear an oath of allegiance to the king.)*
3. What happened to Mary Dyer the first time she was sentenced to be hanged? *(She was spared and sent to Rhode Island.)*

 **Ponder**
Is a person who dies for her beliefs, as Mary Dyer did, a hero?

✓ **Question Chart**

DISCUSS

1. What did Mary Dyer and Anne Hutchinson have in common? *(They both spoke out in favor of ideas that opposed the Puritans; both were punished—Mary Dyer was hanged and Anne Hutchinson was banished.)*
2. Why were Quakers hated and persecuted? *(They did not believe in ministers or in swearing allegiance to the king; they believed in equality, tolerance, and thinking for yourself—these were not ideas other people accepted.)*
3. Why do you think there are statues on Boston Common today honoring Mary Dyer and Anne Hutchinson? *(They exemplify American values of independent thinking and standing up for your beliefs.)*

WRITE

Have students suppose they are friends of Mary Dyer. Her life will be spared if she agrees to leave Massachusetts. Students may write letters, giving their opinions of what she should do: stand up for what she believes? leave Massachusetts forever?

LITERACY LINKS

Words to Discuss

martyr	oath of allegiance
Quaker	cat-o'-nine-tails

Have students use a dictionary and context to determine the meanings of the words. Ask them to make a word web with *Quaker* in the middle. Ask students to explain the connection between each of the other words and *Quaker*. Have them expand the web by adding other words from the chapter.

Reading Skills
Understanding Rhetorical Devices

Have students identify the three paragraphs in the chapter (paragraphs 4, 5, and 6) where the author addresses the reader directly as "you." For each example, ask these questions.
INFERRING

• Why do you think Joy Hakim chooses to talk to you directly in this paragraph? *(4—to make sure the reader understands the connection between church and government in* the 17th century and what happens when people think for themselves; 5—to emphasize the unpopularity of the Quakers; 6—to involve readers in the Puritans' response to Mary Dyer's challenge to their authority)

• Do you think this is a good technique? Why? *(Responses will vary.)*

Of Witches and Dinosaurs

Puritan religious fervor flamed into suspicion among neighbors and mass hysteria. This tragic period led to false accusations, witch trials, and hangings.

ASK

1. Why did people think Elizabeth Parris, Abigail Williams, and other young girls were bewitched? *(They made animal noises and said silly things in church; they also said three women had bewitched them.)*

2. How did the girls spread witch fever? *(They accused people of putting spells on them; more and more people started accusing neighbors of being witches.)*

3. What was the result of the witch trials? *(Twenty people and two dogs were put to death.)*

◎ Ponder

What would it be like to live during a time when neighbors spy on neighbors and children spy on parents?

☑ Question Chart

DISCUSS

1. Why does the author say, "we are all descendants of the Puritans"? *(because many of America's best laws and ideas come from Puritans)*

2. Why does Joy Hakim say, "The judges were scared, like everyone else."? *(No one knew who would be accused of witchcraft next.)*

3. What was the "sad lesson" that was learned by the Puritans at Salem? *(That hysteria should not be substituted for good reason; Puritan judges and courts could make mistakes and condemn innocent people.)*

WRITE

Have students write a caption for the illustration on page 78. What is going on? What are the people doing? Who are the men in black? What is the overall mood?

L I T E R A C Y   L I N K S

Words to Discuss

witchery	witch finder
witchcraft	hysteria

Have students use a dictionary as well as the context of the chapter to determine the meanings of the words. Ask: Which two words mean "what witches do?" Which word describes a person's job? Which word describes the situation in Salem and other towns during the witch trials?

Reading Skills
Understanding Text Organization

Point out that the chapter has two distinct parts. Ask these questions. SYNTHESIZING

- What is the subject of the first part of the chapter? *(what the Puritans were like; examples of their self-righteousness)*

- Where does the second part begin? *(page 78, "But the Puritans had a big problem.")*

- What is the subject of the second part? *(witchcraft; Salem witch trials)*

- Why does the chapter end on a hopeful note? *(Some people apologized; the people who died were cleared; belief in witchcraft ended; people learn from mistakes.)*

Skills Connection
Math

How many people were tried as witches? *(100)* How many were *not* put to death? *(80)* Later, one judge apologized and the court cleared the names of those who had been killed. How many names were cleared? *(20)*

Connecticut, New Hampshire, and Maine

Land hunger and a growing population caused more and more colonists to encroach on Native American lands. At first Indians thought they were sharing the land with the settlers; the settlers believed they had a right to full control of it.

ASK

1. Where did Thomas Hooker and his 100 followers move to when they left Massachusetts? *(west to the Connecticut River valley)*

2. Why did other people from Massachusetts move to Connecticut? *(Massachusetts was crowded; there was better land in Connecticut.)*

3. What were the Fundamental Orders? *(the constitution of the Connecticut River colony)*

4. What land did the king of England give to his friends John Mason and Ferdinando Gorges? *(land that became the colony of New Hampshire and Maine—part of Massachusetts)*

Ponder
What is conservation? Will Europeans go on to conserve the resources in America?

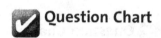 **Question Chart**

DISCUSS

1. The Fundamental Orders established a democratic state controlled by "substantial" citizens. What does *substantial* mean? *(people with property—money or land)*

2. How did European settlers tend to treat the land once they took it from Native Americans? *(cut down trees, filled in swamps, killed animals and birds)*

3. What actions of the king of England show that he felt he owned New England? *(He gave a charter to the Connecticut colony and gave large amounts of land to two of his friends.)*

WRITE

Have students write an ad to attract English settlers to New Hampshire. They can use the map and illustrations on page 82 for help. Challenge them to incorporate as much information about life in New England from the page as possible.

L I T E R A C Y   L I N K S

Words to Discuss

colonization   proprietor
charter   governor

Discuss: What connection do these words have? *(A charter granted by the king was necessary for colonization; a governor or proprietor was responsible for the colony.)* Write *colonization* on the board and have students list its root word *(colony)* and related words *(colonial, colonist, colonize, colonizer).*

Reading Skills
Comparing and Contrasting

Have students read page 84 and then compare/contrast Indian and European views of ownership and use of land. (Ownership: *Europeans believed in individual ownership of land. Indians believed land was to be used by the whole tribe, not owned by individuals.* Use: *Europeans believed owners could change the land to suit their uses; Indians believed people should live in harmony with the land.)* CONNECTING

Skills Connection
Geography

Refer students to the map on page 82. Have them distinguish the three settlements in Connecticut and draw conclusions about why these locations were chosen. *(New London, New Haven, and Hartford are all located on the coast or on a major river. Settlers could travel and transport goods by water.)*

King Philip's War

Indian resentment of English settlements spreading over New England flared into war: first in 1636 with the Pequot War and then in 1675 and 1676 with King Philip's War.

ASK

1. How long did the peace last between the Wampanoag and the English settlers in New England? *(more than 50 years)*
2. How did the English destroy the Pequot fort and defeat the Pequot? *(They surrounded and burned the fort, killing those inside and enslaving those who survived.)*
3. How did English treatment of Metacom's brother help bring on King Philip's War? *(Resentment of English insults to Metacom's brother helped Metacom unite tribes against the English.)*
4. What was the fate of Indians who survived the English victory over the Wampanoag? *(They were sold into slavery in West Indies or Spain.)*

◉ **Ponder**
The author says, "Some of the settlers now feared all Indians." What do you think the result of such fear can be?

✔ **Question Chart**

DISCUSS

1. On page 85 the author says, "There were some—Indians and English—who saw trouble ahead." Do you see trouble ahead between the two? *(Students should predict that just as in Jamestown, the Indians would eventually resent the loss of their land to settlers.)*
2. What were the immediate and underlying causes of the Pequot War and King Philip's War? *(immediate—attacks on English settlers by Indians; murder of Sassamon, a Christian Indian; underlying—loss of land to English settlers and destruction of land)*
3. Have students read the account of Mary Rowlandson's capture by Indians during King Philip's War on Resource 8 (TG page 83) and answer the questions.

WRITE

Have students imagine they are newspaper reporters assigned to write an article on the impact of King Philip's War on settlers and Indians. Remind students to use information from the margin notes and picture captions as well as the text.

L I T E R A C Y   L I N K S

Words to Discuss

retaliate   treaty
revenge   disunity

Have students use a dictionary as well as context to determine the meanings of the words. Discuss: Which word would *not* be used in an account of King Philip's War? *(treaty)* Which word describes a reason the Indians lost the war? *(disunity)*

Reading Skills
Evaluating Point of View

Have students list the words the author uses to describe the Indian-settler conflict in New England. *(wiped out, horrible, executed, revenge, massacred, scalpings, torched villages, incredibly brutal, sold into slavery)* Then ask students to write a sentence explaining their opinion of the author's point of view about this conflict. *(She seems to be critical of both sides.)* ANALYZING

Skills Connection
History

Massasoit asked the General Court in Plymouth to give English names to his two sons, Wamsutta and Metacom. The boys were named for two ancient kings of Greece, Alexander and Philip. Have volunteers research these ancient leaders, and present brief reports to the class.

The Indians Win This One

In 1680 the Indians of New Mexico united in rebellion against the Spanish missionaries and colonists who had taken over their land. Organized by Popé, the Indians drove the Spanish out. It would be 12 years before the Spanish reconquered New Mexico.

ASK

1. Who was Popé and what did he do? *(a religious leader who united Indians to drive out Spanish colonists in New Mexico in 1680)*

2. What made Popé's task difficult? *(Indians were not used to acting in a united way; they spoke different languages.)*

3. How did Popé trick the Spanish? *(He arranged to have false plans of the revolution fall into Spanish hands.)*

⊙ Ponder
The Spaniards and Pueblo Indians will continue to "misunderstand each other." What do you think will be the result of that?

DISCUSS

1. How did the arrival of the Spaniards change the Indians' lives? *(Spanish priests tried to ban the Indians' religion and convert them to Christianity. Spaniards imprisoned and sometimes killed Indians who refused.)*

2. Why were the Pueblos willing to follow Popé against the Spaniards? *(The Spaniards had tried to destroy Indian religions and they had executed Indian religious leaders.)*

3. What does the chapter title mean? *(The title compares the eastern Indians—who failed to drive away the English settlers—with Popé and the southwestern Indians who succeeded in driving the Spanish out of New Mexico.)*

4. What was *la Reconquista* and why did it succeed? *(Reconquest—the return of the Spaniards to New Mexico in 1692; it succeeded because Popé had died and the Pueblos were no longer united.)*

✓ Question Chart

WRITE

Have partners write a dialogue between Popé and a Pueblo Indian in 1680. Popé is trying to convince the Pueblo to join the uprising. What arguments would Popé use? What questions might the other Indian have?

L I T E R A C Y   L I N K S

Words to Discuss

reconquest	uprising
kiva	mission
kachina	conversion
unity	

Have students write *Pueblo Uprising* and *Reconquest* on a sheet of paper and then list the words and phrases that apply to each heading in the appropriate column. *(Possible responses: Pueblo uprising—kiva, kachina, unity; Reconquest—conversion, mission)*

Reading Skills
Summarizing

Tell students that *summarizing* is restating the main points of something. Introduce the skill by asking volunteers to describe the plot of a favorite movie in a few sentences. Ask why summaries are useful. *(They save time; they quickly give an idea of what something's about.)* Reread the chapter and help students summarize by asking the following questions about paragraph 3 on page 88:

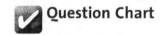

• What is the main idea of paragraph 3? What are the important details? *(Main idea: Spanish invaders were cruel to people of the pueblos. Details: they forced Indians to grow crops, convert to Christianity, pay taxes, clean house, do heavy work.)*

Have students summarize what Popé did in Chapter 23. *(trained as leader; freed from Spanish dungeon by Indians; united Pueblos and Apaches; fooled Spaniards about date of the attack; forced Spaniards back to Mexico)*
ANALYZING

THINKING ABOUT THE THEMES

The following questions will help students relate the book's themes to the content of Part 4. You may wish to use the questions for classroom discussion or have students answer them in written form.

1. What changes did the Wampanoag face when the first English settlers arrived in what they called Plymouth? *(sharing their land; agreeing to a peace treaty)*

2. How did the Puritans and Spanish feel about religious diversity? *(Neither tolerated diversity. Both tried to force everyone in their colony to follow the same religion— Puritanism or Catholicism.)*

3. What were some of the conflicts that tore apart New England in the 17th century? *(between Quakers and Puritans over religious beliefs; between Indians and colonists who wanted land; accusations of witchcraft in Salem)*

4. Draw students' attention to the themes that have been posted around the room. Give them the opportunity to explore the relevance of these themes to Part 4. Accept choices that are supported by sound reasoning.

ASSESSING PART 4

Use Check-Up 4 (TG page 72) to assess student learning.

NOTE FROM JOY HAKIM

Set up a TV talk show. The moderator is a news reporter; the guests are experts on an event of the time. Have your "experts" prepare statements and then expect to answer "call-in questions" from the classroom audience.

PROJECTS AND ACTIVITIES

▶ Colonial Legacies

Tell students to imagine that the Puritans and the Quakers of Massachusetts Bay Colony left a will, passing on the best of their ideas to future Americans. Create a class version of the will using chart paper. Start with *We hereby leave to future generations:* and list the legacies in two columns, one for Puritans, one for Quakers.

▶ Massachusetts Bay Colony Newspaper

Write the following headlines on the chalkboard: *Who's in Charge in Salem?*; *Our Loss Is Providence's Gain*; *Banished!*; *Fundamental Orders Explained.* Assign small groups a headline, and have them collect facts for the news story. To organize their facts, have students divide a sheet of paper into sections labeled *Who? What? Where? When? Why?* and *How?*

▶ Write a Dialogue

Have students work in pairs to imagine a conversation between Popé and Metacom about the settlers on their land. What advice for Metacom would Popé have? What complaints about the Spanish and English would they share?

▶ Fact Sheet: The Thirteen English Colonies

Have partners fill in facts about Rhode Island, Connecticut, and New Hampshire on Resource 3 (TG page 78).

▶ Map of the English Colonies

Distribute Resource 9 (TG page 84) and have students identify the colonies they have studied in Part 4.

▶ Timeline

Have students update their timelines with additional information from Part 4.

★★ FACTS TO SHARE ★★

Indians taught the English settlers how to prepare a nutritious fast food, light enough to be carried on long trips. First they parched corn in the ashes of a fire; then they ground the corn into a powder. The settlers made their own version and called it *journey cake*, because it was good for a day's journey.

Founding the Middle Colonies

Settlement of the Middle Colonies began in New Netherland (later New York) in the early 1600s. The founders and settlers of the Middle Colonies avoided some of the mistakes of earlier colonists. A diverse group, they were changing the cultures they had brought with them from Europe—experimenting with religious freedom and representative government.

SETTING GOALS

The goals for students in Part 5 are to:
- understand the role of national rivalries in founding the Middle Colonies.
- understand different types of colonies.
- investigate the effects of the English Civil War on the American colonies.
- understand how England's class system spurred English colonization in America.
- examine the lives and achievements of William Penn and Benjamin Franklin.

GETTING INTERESTED

1. Have students preview Chapters 24-29 by looking at titles, headings, illustrations, captions, margin notes, and quotations. Ask them to speculate about why these are called "middle" colonies.

2. Have students use the map on page 94 to tell which colonies make up the Middle Colonies. *(New York, New Jersey, Pennsylvania, Delaware)* Verify their answers using the map on page 99.

3. Based on chapter titles, illustrations, and margin notes, ask students to identify some of the people they will be reading about in these chapters. *(Henry Hudson, Peter Stuyvesant, Duke of York, King Charles I, Oliver Cromwell, William Penn, Charles II, Ben Franklin)* Ask: Which names are familiar to you? Which are names of people in England? *(Responses will vary.)*

Working with Timelines
Have students add to their ongoing timelines. Point out that for these chapters they will be adding dates later in the 1600s. Suggest that some students create biographical timelines of people they have met so far in their reading, including the people they will meet in these chapters, especially William Penn and Benjamin Franklin.

Using Maps
Have students turn again to the map of the English Colonies on page 94. Ask: What mountain range stretches from Georgia to northern Massachusetts (Maine)? *(Appalachian Mountains)* How might these mountains have affected settlement in the West? *(They blocked settlers who wanted to move west.)*

What's a Colony?

Historians divide the 13 English colonies into New England, Middle, and Southern Colonies. It was the Dutch who began the settlement of the Middle Colonies.

ASK

1. Why were places such as Massachusetts and Connecticut called colonies? *(Another country—England—claimed the land and had power over the people who lived there.)*
2. Why was Henry Hudson exploring the river (named for him) in 1609? *(He was looking for the Northwest Passage to the Pacific Ocean.)*
3. Why did Jonas Michaelius write a letter to the Dutch West India Company in 1628? *(The company's promises about life in New Netherland weren't kept.)*

◎ **Ponder**
If our society didn't use metal and paper money, what goods would we use to buy things?

✔ **Question Chart**

DISCUSS

1. Write *colony* on the board and ask students to brainstorm a definition. Compare their definitions to the one on page 92.
2. Why were the Dutch interested in colonizing America? *(They thought the fur trade might pay off.)*
3. What were some similarities between the Dutch West India Company and the Virginia Company, which had sent English settlers to Jamestown? *(Both companies owned colonies and both gave out false information to attract colonists.)*

WRITE

Have students look at the picture on page 93 and ask them to write a sentence or two telling what each person in the illustration is doing.

LITERACY LINKS

Words to Discuss

colony   landlord
renters   mint

Have students use a dictionary and context to determine the meanings of the words. Have students write sentences explaining how each of the other words is connected to *colony*. *(A country that established colonies was like a* landlord; *the colonies were like* renters. *Colonies were not allowed to* mint *their own money.)*

Reading Skills
Identifying Primary and Secondary Sources

Primary sources give firsthand information about a subject. These materials—artifacts, diaries, photographs, legal documents—are records of events made by eyewitnesses. *Secondary sources* are descriptions or interpretations of events by people who weren't eyewitnesses. Have students identify the primary and secondary sources in the chapter and explain their choices. *(Primary: seal, coins and bills, Michaelius's letter—they were made or written at the time. Secondary: picture on page 93—it was painted after the time.)* ANALYZING

Skills Connection
Mathematics

Make sure students understand what is meant by a *generation*. First have students answer the question on page 92 about how long colonial times lasted. *(169 years)* Then have them divide by seven to find the number of years in a generation. *(a little more than 24 years)*

Silvernails and Big Tub

Both Holland and Sweden founded colonies in America in the 1600s. The colonies had colorful leaders, Peter Stuyvesant and Johan Prinze.

ASK

1. Why did the Dutch think they had a claim to land in America? *(because of Hudson's voyage in 1609)*
2. Which two nations established colonies located between the New England colonies and Virginia? *(The Netherlands and Sweden)*
3. What was the major item of trade in New Netherland and New Sweden? *(furs)*
4. Joy Hakim's states on page 98, "It was said you could hear 18 different languages being spoken in . . . New Amsterdam." How do you explain the diverse population of New Amsterdam? *(ships came to the harbor from faraway places)*

 **Ponder**
How might our country be different today if the Dutch and Swedes had held on to their colonies?

✔ **Question Chart**

DISCUSS

1. Why do you suppose men like Peter Stuyvesant and Johan Prinze were chosen to run colonies in America? *(They were strong leaders and no one would take advantage of them.)*
2. What were Peter Stuyvesant's views on religious freedom? *(He didn't believe in religious freedom; he saw no reason to tolerate any religion other than his own.)*
3. Why did the Dutch and Swedes lose their American colonies? *(National rivalry for colonial power led to the Dutch takeover of New Sweden and then the English takeover of New Netherland)*

WRITE

Ask students to imagine they are reporters assigned to interview Old Silvernails after his conquest of New Sweden. Have them write a list of questions they would ask and then write his probable responses. Students may work in pairs.

L I T E R A C Y   L I N K S

Words to Discuss

pelts
Dutch Reformed Church
elected councilors
log cabin

Ask: Which words refer to New Netherland, New Sweden, or both? *(New Netherland: Dutch Reformed Church, elected councilors; New Sweden: autocrat, log cabin; Both: pelts)*

Reading Skills
Interpreting Point of View

Have students decide whether Joy Hakim's view of Peter Stuyvesant is positive or negative. Ask students to use specific words and phrases to defend their opinion. *(Possible responses: Negative—hard-swearing, bigot, did not tolerate other religions; Positive—tough, good at running things, popular after defeating New Sweden)* INFERRING

Meeting Individual Needs
Visual Learners

Direct students' attention to the three illustrations of New Amsterdam on page 97. Ask:

• Which two views show New Amsterdam from opposite sides? *(the large picture and bottom picture)*
• Which two pictures show the tip of Manhattan? *(the small pictures)*
• In the bottom picture, where is Brooklyn Heights? *(at the top of the picture, across the East River)*

West to Jersey

When the British seized New Netherland in 1664, the Duke of York controlled the land and named part of it New York. The other part, which later became New Jersey, he gave to two of his friends.

ASK

1. Look at the chapter title. Who would be moving west to get to New Jersey? *(people in New York, or people in Europe)*
2. How did proprietors profit from the colonies? *(They collected a tax from settlers called a "quit rent.")*
3. What happened to East Jersey and West Jersey when the king took over from the proprietors? *(The colony became New Jersey and was assigned a royal governor; the colonists kept their assembly and made their own laws.)*
4. What are the nationalities of some of the settlers who came to New York and New Jersey? *(Finnish, German, Swedish, English)*

⊙ Ponder
European rulers treated America as their personal property, dividing it up with no thought of the Indians. If you were a settler who was sympathetic to the Indians, what would you have told King Charles?

✔ Question Chart

DISCUSS

1. Have students locate the city of New York on the map on page 99. Ask the class to brainstorm reasons why this would become an important city. *(access to the Atlantic Ocean and to the Hudson River)*
2. Why do you think the charter for New Jersey attracted settlers to the colony? *(It provided for representative government and freedom of religion.)*
3. Why was the Duke of York interested in promoting the slavery of Africans? *(His company controlled the British slave trade; the colonists could become new customers for slaves.)*
4. What does Joy Hakim mean when she asks you to "look up" to find the frontier today? *(In this century, space is the frontier.)*

WRITE

Have students imagine they are settlers in what was to become New Jersey. Have them write a letter home to a relative or friend explaining why their colony's charter is "the best."

LITERACY LINKS

Words to Discuss

assembly	royal governor
proprietor	quit rent

Have students use context and prior knowledge to define the words. Ask: Which of these words describe colonial government? *(assembly, proprietor, royal governor)* Which word describes what a colonist paid to a proprietor? *(quit rent)*

Reading Skills
Comparing and Contrasting

Have students read the first two paragraphs on page 101 to compare and contrast the government of New Jersey with that of the Massachusetts Bay Colony. Ask these questions.
CONNECTING

- What freedoms did people enjoy in New Jersey and not in Massachusetts? *(Freedom of religion; all males could vote for assembly members.)*

- How would these freedoms affect population growth? *(People who valued freedom would come to New Jersey.)*

- What event of 1675-1676 might have discouraged settlement in Massachusetts? *(King Philip's War)*

Cromwell and Charles

A struggle for control of the English government between the Stuart kings and the Puritans led by Oliver Cromwell ended in a victory for the monarchy and spurred settlement of the Middle Colonies.

ASK

1. Why were the Puritans called "roundheads"? *(They wore their hair short at a time when other men wore their hair long.)*

2. Why does Joy Hakim want us to remember the year 1649? *(King Charles I was overthrown, proving that people can change their government.)*

3. What was the Restoration? *(the period when the monarchy was restored under Charles II)*

4. What happened to the Puritans during the Restoration? *(They were mistreated; some were killed; many came to America.)*

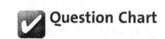 **Ponder**
If the Puritans had kept power in England, would the colonies have gained more control over their own affairs?

✔️ **Question Chart**

DISCUSS

1. From what you know about the settlers in New England and Virginia, why does it make sense that in the English Civil War, New England colonists sided with the Roundheads and Virginia colonists sided with the Cavaliers? *(Many people in New England were Puritans; Jamestown was settled by gentlemen who were natural allies of the Cavaliers.)*

2. What were some of the things the Puritans did under Oliver Cromwell? *(beheaded the king; closed theaters, burned churches, destroyed art, and killed people for their beliefs)*

3. How did the English Civil War and the Restoration affect the English colonies in America? *(King Charles II rewarded people who were loyal to him with land in America, which resulted in more colonies; many people left England for America.)*

WRITE

On page 103, Joy Hakim says of the English Civil War that "kings came back. But it [the War] wasn't a failure." Have students write a paragraph explaining why they agree or disagree with the statement.

L I T E R A C Y   L I N K S

Words to Discuss

Protectorate   **Restoration**
Cavalier

Have students use a dictionary and context to define the words. Ask: which words apply to Oliver Cromwell, and which apply to the king? (Protectorate—*government of Oliver Cromwell*; Cavalier—*supporters of the king*; Restoration—*the return of rule by a king*)

Reading Skills
Interpreting Sequence

As students reread Chapter 27, have them chart the sequence of events in the English Civil War. Pose the following questions to help students gather information from the chapter. CONNECTING

• The two sides were known as Roundheads and Cavaliers. Who were they? *(Puritans and supporters of King Charles I)*

• When was Charles I beheaded? *(1649)*

• What was the Protectorate? *(Puritan government under Oliver Cromwell)*

• What happened under Cromwell's rule? *(Anglicans and Catholics killed, churches and art destroyed, theaters closed)*

• When did Oliver Cromwell die? *(1658)*

• What brought about the restoration of King Charles II? *(Puritans lost power when Cromwell's son took over)*

William the Wise

William Penn, a Quaker, founded Pennsylvania as a haven for persecuted Quakers and people of all religions.

ASK

1. Why did King Charles II give William Penn land in America? *(to pay off a debt to William Penn's father)*

2. How did William Penn reach out to the Indians? *(He wrote to them saying he wanted to live together in peace; he proposed a league of peace.)*

3. How did the colony of Delaware begin? *(The three southeastern counties of Pennsylvania asked for their own assembly and Penn granted the request, leading the way to a separate colony of Delaware.)*

◎ Ponder

Joy Hakim says on page 106: "Wealthy people didn't want things to change." Is that statement true of William Penn? Why or why not?

✓ Question Chart

DISCUSS

1. How did Penn's Quaker beliefs help to make him one of the best leaders of a colony? *(Quakers believed in treating people equally—including Indians—and respected all religions; they refused to go to war.)*

2. Explain the difference between toleration and equality in the English colonies. *(toleration—religious freedom but no political rights unless you were part of the majority religion; equality—religious freedom and the right to vote or hold office)*

3. Have students use Resource 10 (TG page 85) to compare population growth in Pennsylvania to that of other colonies between 1680 and 1740.

WRITE

Read aloud the excerpts from Penn's letter to the Indians on page 107. Have students assume the role of colonists and write a diary entry expressing an opinion about what Penn has said.

LITERACY LINKS

Words to Discuss

class system
conscientious objector

Have students use context to define the words. Ask: What word is a root of *conscientious*? *(conscience)* How does that help you understand what *conscientious objector* means? *(A conscientious objector follows his or her conscience, which objects to fighting, and refuses to fight.)*

Reading Skills
Interpreting Character

Have students decide whether William Penn would be as good a leader in today's world as he was in his own time. QUESTIONING

- Brainstorm character traits of a good leader.

- Discuss the qualities of William Penn as a leader of Pennsylvania. *(believed in treating everyone equally and respecting all religions; treated Indians as equals; generous and fair)*

- Assign teams to create a list of questions to ask William Penn to help them decide if he would be an effective leader today. *(Students should ask questions such as, How would you share your power? What would you do if someone broke the rules? Who would you take advice from?)*

- Have teams exchange lists and answer each other's questions.

Ben Franklin

Benjamin Franklin was always striving for self-improvement. He epitomizes the American Dream: rising from poverty to make unique and lasting contributions in science, technology, and politics.

ASK

1. What did Franklin do with the money he saved by becoming a vegetarian? *(He bought books.)*

2. Why did Benjamin Franklin leave Boston? *(He ran away from his job as an apprentice to his brother.)*

3. How is Benjamin Franklin's life an example of Joy Hakim's statement on page 106: "In America, with hard work, many poor people would rise to the top." *(He started out poor, worked very hard, and achieved great things, among them helping to found a new nation.)*

Ponder
Looking over Benjamin Franklin's life, what adjectives would you use to describe him?

Question Chart

DISCUSS

1. Joy Hakim says on page 110, "I think you would have liked him [Franklin]." Do you think so? Why? *(Responses may include mention of Franklin's humor and wit, his hatred for pompous people, his inventiveness.)*

2. Distribute Resource 11 (TG page 86). Divide the class into small groups and ask students to suppose that they are on a committee to rename their school. Tell them that each team is in favor of naming the school in honor of Benjamin Franklin. Based on Resource 11, have each team prepare a statement giving reasons for naming the school for Franklin. *(Responses will vary.)*

WRITE

Have students write an advertisement for one of Benjamin Franklin's inventions or the almanac shown on page 110. Tell students that they are writing the ad to the people of Franklin's time.

L I T E R A C Y   L I N K S

Words to Discuss

apprentice	almanac
industrious	countrified

Have students use a dictionary and context to define the words. Ask volunteers to explain how each word relates to Franklin's life and achievements.

Reading Skills
Interpreting a Primary Source

Sourcebook: Read aloud the introduction to Source #9 and selected entries from the *Almanack*. Ask these questions. CONNECTING

• Why was *Poor Richard's Almanack* important to colonial readers? *(They needed its information and enjoyed its humor and common sense.)*

• Which sayings on page 113 do you recognize? What do they mean?

Dictate different sayings from the *Almanack* to students, and invite teams to explain what they mean.

Skills Connection
Geography

Have students use Resource 2 (TG page 77) to calculate the distance from Boston to Philadelphia. *(almost 300 miles)* Ask: Traveling on foot, what colonies would Franklin have passed through? Which were New England Colonies and which were Middle Colonies? *(Rhode Island and Connecticut—New England; New York, New Jersey—Middle Colonies)*

THINKING ABOUT THE THEMES

The following questions will help students relate the book's themes to the content of Part 5. You may wish to use the questions for classroom discussion or have students answer them in written form.

1. Why was the population of the Middle Colonies so diverse? *(tolerance of different religious and political views; the economic advantages of the fur trade)*

2. Following the defeat of the Puritans in the English Civil War, what changes came to the Middle Colonies? *(King Charles II gave generous land grants to his supporters.)*

3. How did continuing religious conflict in England and other countries affect the Middle Colonies? *(Conflict caused many people to come to the Middle Colonies.)*

4. Draw students' attention to the themes that have been posted around the room. Give them the opportunity to explore the relevance of these themes to Part 5. Accept choices that are supported by sound reasoning.

ASSESSING PART 5

Use Check-Up 5 (TG page 73) to assess student learning.

NOTE FROM JOY HAKIM

I believe all teachers need to think across disciplines and concern themselves with language—even in a history book. You'll find these books give you a rich opportunity to study vocabulary. Ask your students to search for ten words they didn't know, define them, and use each in a sentence. Then have a vocabulary bee.

PROJECTS AND ACTIVITIES

▶ **Debate: Middle Colonies vs. New England Colonies**

Have students take *Pro* or *Con* positions on the following topic: *Resolved:* That the Middle Colonies were a better place to live than the New England Colonies. *(Pro: the Middle Colonies were more tolerant of different religions, more representative in their government, less restrictive. Con: New England colonies placed more emphasis on leading a good life, on education, and on serving as an example to all nations.)*

▶ **Pennsylvania Postcards**

Have students choose an illustration from Chapters 28 or 29 and imagine it is a picture postcard. Ask them to write a message to a friend in England explaining the picture and connecting it to life in the colony.

▶ **A Colonial Almanac**

Have students discuss what an almanac is and what a colonial almanac contained. Reread selections from *Poor Richard's Almanack (Sourcebook,* Source #9). Have individual students contribute an entry appropriate for colonial times in one of these categories: witty sayings, wise advice, comments on events, astounding facts.

▶ **Fact Sheet: The Thirteen English Colonies**

Have students add information about the Middle Colonies to their copies of Resource 3 (TG page 78).

▶ **Map of the English Colonies**

Distribute Resource 9 (TG page 84) and have students identify the colonies they have studied in Part 5.

▶ **Timeline**

Have students update their timelines with additional information from Part 5. Interested students can start a timeline for the life of William Penn or Benjamin Franklin.

★★ FACTS TO SHARE ★★

Benjamin Franklin created the first postal delivery system in Philadelphia as well as the first Dead Letter office. Not only did he devise ways to speed up the delivery of overseas mail, he hired extra riders to improve domestic delivery. He even helped Canada with its mail system.

Founding the Southern Colonies

In *The Present State of Virginia*, Hugh Jones wrote of some colonists in Virginia: "They live in the same manner, dress after the same fashion, and behave themselves exactly as the gentry in London." Southerners who identified closely with England were the leaders of their colonies. And slavery affected every aspect of life in the southern colonies.

SETTING GOALS

The goals for students in Part 6 are to:
- understand how tolerance of diversity advanced in the colonies.
- discover why slavery became widespread in Virginia.
- understand life on a plantation and the lives of indentured servants, small farmers, and slaves.
- learn about life in two important southern cities: Williamsburg and Charleston.
- understand an early independence movement in North Carolina.

GETTING INTERESTED

1. Have students preview Chapters 30-36 by looking at titles, headings, illustrations, captions, margin notes, and quotations. Remind them they have already learned about one southern colony, Virginia. Ask: Which Southern Colonies have now joined Virginia? *(Maryland, South Carolina, and North Carolina)*

2. Have students compare the New England town on page 66 to the southern plantation on page 123. Ask students to point out similarities and differences. *(Similarities: well laid out; met the needs of people living there. Differences: towns had businesses and a meeting house; plantations were self-sufficient farms with housing for slaves.)* Explain to students that they will be learning more about the conflicts within a society with large numbers of enslaved people.

Working with Timelines
On the board, write the names and dates of the founding of the Southern Colonies—Virginia, 1607; Maryland, 1633; Carolinas, 1663; Georgia, 1732. Ask students to add these dates to their timelines. (Explain that because Georgia was founded so much later, it is covered in Part 7.)

Using Maps
Have students turn to the map of the English Colonies on page 94 and note the ones they have studied so far *(Virginia, New England and Middle Colonies)* and then locate the Southern Colonies: Virginia, Maryland, South Carolina, North Carolina, and Georgia.

Maryland's Form of Toleration

Although the aristocratic Catholic Calvert family founded Maryland as a haven for persecuted Catholics as well as for Protestants, non-Christians were excluded.

ASK

1. What was the Calvert family's dream for Maryland? *(a colony "founded on religious freedom" where Catholics and Protestants could live in harmony)*
2. What kind of government did Maryland have? *(representative government)*
3. Who had to "keep quiet or leave Maryland" because the Toleration Act did not include them? *(Jews, atheists, Christians who asked too many questions)*

🌀 **Ponder**
Why was Maryland's Toleration Act a "landmark" if it didn't give complete freedom to everyone?

✅ **Question Chart**

DISCUSS

1. How would you compare the Calverts' reasons for founding a colony with those of William Penn? *(Both intended their colonies to be a haven for people of their own religions; both welcomed other religions—Calverts only welcomed other Christians; Penn tolerated more diversity.)*
2. How would you compare the Calverts' and William Penn's attitudes toward government? *(Both established representative governments in their colonies.)*
3. Why did many apprentices and servants run away in colonial Maryland? *(mistreatment at the hands of the people to whom they were "bound out")*

WRITE

Ask students to imagine they are "bound out" until age 21 to an employer. Ask them to write a diary entry expressing their opinions of the arrangement. Ask them to calculate how many more years they have to serve, based on their current age.

L I T E R A C Y   L I N K S

Words to Discuss

| Toleration Act | bound out |
| religious freedom | atheist |

Have students use context and prior knowledge to define the words. Ask students to imagine they have been offered a chance to plan a colony on Mars. Ask them to use each of these words in a description of how their colony will (or will not) be organized.

Reading Skills
Evaluating Graphic Aids

Have students look at the illustrations on pages 114-116. Ask the following questions. CONNECTING

- What people are shown? *(George Calvert and Charles I's wife; Charles Calvert and slave; glassblower and apprentice)*
- Which people are working? *(glassblower and apprentice)*
- What do the pictures add to the chapter? *(They show people mentioned in the chapter; they show work in the colony.)*

Skills Connection
Geography

Have students compare the map of Maryland on page 115 with John Smith's map of Virginia on page 23. Read the caption on page 115 and then ask students to answer the question posed in the caption. *(size and location of hills and rivers south, north, and west of Chesapeake Bay)*

Carry Me Back to Ole Virginny

Dominated by a land-owning aristocracy, Virginia developed around an agricultural economy whose major crop was tobacco. For labor, many small farmers and all plantation owners turned to slavery, which made Africans the single largest group in Virginia.

ASK

1. Why did the importation of African slaves hurt yeoman farmers? *(Yeoman farmers couldn't compete with large plantations worked by slaves; the tobacco grown by yeomen farmers was more expensive than tobacco grown by slave labor.)*

2. What laws did Virginians pass regarding slaves and black people? *(Laws made it illegal to free slaves, to educate black people, and for black people to own land.)*

3. What are some problems with an economy dependent on a single crop like tobacco? *(When crop prices are high, everything is fine; when prices drop, the bottom falls out: there are no other products to sell.)*

Ponder
Some slave owners tried to justify slavery by telling themselves that it existed in ancient societies. Was that a good reason to continue slavery?

DISCUSS

1. Why do you suppose Virginians thought it was necessary to pass slave laws? *(They believed the only way to maintain slavery and their way of life was to deny enslaved people all rights—to freedom, education, choice of where to work or live.)*

2. Why did tobacco farmers need lots of land? *(Because nothing grows well on land that has been planted with tobacco, the land needs to rest every few years.)*

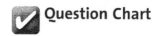 **Question Chart**

WRITE

Have students imagine they are 18th-century lawyers in Virginia. They are defending a plantation owner who has defied the law by teaching an enslaved person to read. Students should write a brief speech explaining why the plantation owner should not be punished.

L I T E R A C Y   L I N K S

Words to Discuss

paradox

Tell students that a paradox is a puzzle because it often appears to be contradictory or beyond explanation. Discuss what the paradox was in Colonial Virginia. *(Some of the people who thought and wrote most about freedom were slave-owning Virginians.)* How is it possible to believe in liberty as well as slavery? Ask: Have you ever had contradictory feelings or thoughts at the same time?

Reading Skills
Evaluating Text Features

Have students look at the slave auction notice and caption on page 119 and the margin note on page 120. Then ask the following questions. ANALYZING

• How does the auction notice add to our understanding of the evils of slavery? *(It shows the ugly details of buying and selling human beings.)*

• What information do you get from the margin note? *(Not all people supported slavery; some slaves were treated worse than horses.)*

Meeting Individual Needs
Reteaching

Help students understand the impact of tobacco on Virginia. Have them work in pairs to fill in a three-column chart titled *Tobacco's Impact*. The columns should be labeled *Economy, Land*, and *People*. *(Economy: one-crop, tobacco-based; Land: exhausted the soil; large plantations emerged; small farms squeezed out; People: small farmers left or bought slaves; more and more African slaves needed to work on large tobacco plantations)*

The Good Life

A large plantation was like a self-contained village. It produced almost everything its residents needed—housing, food, clothing, education, work, income, and entertainment.

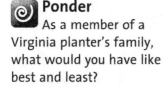

ASK

1. In what way was a plantation like a small village? *(It was self-sufficient—most of the residents' needs could be met right there.)*
2. How were planter's children educated on the plantation? *(taught at home, learned languages, dancing, learned to play musical instrument)*
3. What expectations were there for boys in the family? *(go on to college and later serve in the House of Burgesses, to be a leader)*

Ponder
As a member of a Virginia planter's family, what would you have like best and least?

Question Chart

DISCUSS

1. Why do you think Joy Hakim calls this chapter "The Good Life"? *(She is describing what life was like for the "few lucky enough to be born wealthy.")*
2. Who made the good life possible? How? *(African slaves; they did all the hard work.)*
3. For an understanding of the self-sufficiency of a plantation, have students look at the map on page 123. Ask volunteers to read and explain the labels. Make sure students know the function of each place shown.

WRITE

Ask students to imagine they are writing a guide to the plantation illustrated on page 123. Have them write a short description of the plantation and mention specific buildings and features.

L I T E R A C Y   L I N K S

Words to Discuss

executive	bondman
bondwoman	euphemism

Have students use a dictionary and context to define the words. Then ask: Why did people use the euphemisms *bondman* and *bondwoman* instead of *slave*? *(to avoid embarrassment; to make it sound "nicer")* In what way could *executive* be a euphemism for *slave owner*? *(It's a "nicer" word for someone who's running a business.)*

Reading Skills
Understanding Point of View

Have students read through the chapter and pick out words and phrases that show Joy Hakim's opinion of the "good life." *(for example, privileged, lordly, you need to be intelligent and industrious, hard work; some parts of children's lives are nice; fun [wearing satin gowns and petticoats], some parts uncomfortable [ruffled shirts and high-heeled shoes for company; rigorous education])*
ANALYZING

Skills Connection
Geography

Have students look at the plantation map on page 123 and the map of the Southern Colonies on page 118. Ask: Why were many plantations located on rivers and on the Virginia coast? *(The location made it easier for planters to transport tobacco by ship.)*

Virginia's Capital

Williamsburg was developed as the capital of Virginia. The House of Burgesses, which met there, brought together several men who would one day be founders of the United States.

ASK

1. Why was the capital of Virginia moved from Jamestown to Williamsburg? *(better climate; higher, healthier ground)*
2. What happened in Williamsburg during Public Times in April and October? *(People came there to do business, make laws, consider court cases, see friends, shop.)*
3. Where did many of them go when the Public Times were over? *(back to their plantations)*

DISCUSS

1. Who ruled Virginia? *(an English governor and the House of Burgesses, made up of men who were landowners and who belonged to the Anglican church)*
2. What happened to Virginians' efforts to educate Indians? *(The first plan was ended after three years; in 1723 a permanent school for Indians opened at the College of William and Mary.)*
3. Have students use Resource 10 (TG page 85) to compare the growth of Virginia's population to that of other colonies between 1670 and 1700.

⊚ Ponder
There were people in early colonial times whose lives became very comfortable. What did these people think about the system of rigid classes that existed in England? Would they have been interested in that system? Why or why not?

☑ Question Chart

WRITE

Imagine you have come to Williamsburg during Public Times. Using information on page 127, write a letter to a friend back home about what you have seen and done while you were there.

LITERACY LINKS

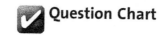

Words to Discuss

tyrant	crown
governor	gentry

Have students use a dictionary and context to define the words. Then ask: Which words refer to a ruler? *(governor, crown)* Which word describes an unfair ruler? *(tyrant)* Which group would fall just below the nobility? *(gentry)*

Reading Skills
Evaluating Word Choice

Have partners reread paragraphs 2-4 on page 126 and identify words and phrases that help them visualize the city of Williamsburg and its people. *(wide, tree-lined street, white spire, neat houses, grassy mall, horses, cows, sheep, stone unicorn, fancy gates, candlelit ballroom, starched linen blouses, silk brocade gowns, boxwood maze garden, peacocks)* Then have partners write several sentences describing in their own words what they have pictured. VISUALIZING

Meeting Individual Needs
Visual Learners

Have students draw pictures of the gardens behind the palace of Williamsburg's governor.

Pretend Some More

Compared to the life of rich plantation owners, life for other Southerners—artisans, small farmers, and slaves—was considerably harder. For some, it was very harsh.

ASK

1. Which children described in this chapter were able to read? *(children of indentured servants and farmers)*
2. Which children were not allowed to learn to read? *(children of slaves)*
3. What evidence can you find in this chapter that there was no freedom of religion in Virginia? *(The law required everyone to go to the Anglican church every Sunday; children could be taken away from parents who chose to worship in a different way.)*

Ponder
Draw students' attention to the illustration at the bottom of page 130. What machine(s) would people "venerate" today?

Question Chart

DISCUSS

1. What was life like for each of the children described? *(indentured servant—lived with the family that bought his labor, worked hard, might be treated badly, might learn to read; poor farmer—lived with own family; some schooling, not enough healthy food to eat; slave—might live with family; could be sold away; not allowed to read or move without the owner's permission.)*
2. What does Joy Hakim mean when she says, "Virginians feel closer to people in England than they do to those in New England." *(Unlike the people of New England, most Virginians belong to the Anglican church; they like English clothing, paintings, furnishings, ideas.)*

WRITE

Have student pairs write a list of questions to ask a child in 18th-century Virginia. Have partners exchange lists and write answers to each other's questions.

LITERACY LINKS

Words to Discuss

indentured servant
apprentice

Have students use a dictionary and the context of the chapter to define the words. Discuss: Would you rather be an apprentice or an indentured servant? *(Responses will vary.)*

Reading Skills
Interpreting Rhetorical Devices

Have students determine how Joy Hakim helps readers imagine they are "in the scene" she is describing. Read aloud the title and first sentence of the chapter and ask these questions. ANALYZING

• From the title and first sentence, what do you notice about this chapter? *(Joy Hakim is telling her reader to pretend; she sets a scene with the reader in it.)*

• What are some of the ways the author helps readers feel that they are part of this chapter? *(She speaks to the reader as "you"; gives specific details about your life, such as who your family is, where you sleep and what clothes you have; your aspirations; what you can and cannot do; predictions about your future.)*

• Which scene and person seem most real to you? Explain. *(Responses will vary.)*

South Carolina: Riches, Rice, Slaves

South Carolina emerged as a highly prosperous colony with an economy based on rice and indigo, grown by slave labor. It had an aristocratic class that held the colony's economic and political power, and the only great city in the South—Charleston.

ASK

1. Who were the Huguenots and why did they come to South Carolina? *(French Protestants who came to escape persecution in France)*
2. What did Charleston and Philadelphia have in common? *(The streets in both cities were planned before any houses were built.)*
3. Why does Joy Hakim say that John Smith would have welcomed the Huguenots in Jamestown? *(The Huguenots had important skills and were hardworking, unlike the English gentlemen who settled Jamestown in 1607.)*
4. What crop made slavery profitable in South Carolina? *(rice)*

◎ Ponder
Where do you go to escape the heat of the summer?

✔ Question Chart

DISCUSS

1. How did the leaders of South Carolina try to attract settlers? *(through a policy of religious tolerance)*
2. Why was Charleston important to South Carolina? *(It was the busiest port in the South, with an elegant social scene; it provided a refuge from disease for the wealthy during the summer months.)*
3. Have students study the graph on Resource 12 (TG page 87) and answer questions about the growth of South Carolina's slave population.

WRITE

Have students start to fill in information about South Carolina on Resource 13 (TG page 88).

LITERACY LINKS

Words to Discuss

indigo   Gullah
Huguenots

Have students use context to define the words. Ask: What are some Gullah words we use in English? *(goober, voodoo, gumbo)* Why do you think indigo was sometimes used as money? *(because it was so valuable)*

Reading Skills
Evaluating Point of View

Read aloud the poem on page 134 as students follow along. Have volunteers reread the poem dramatically, emphasizing the rhythm and rhyme.

Then ask the following questions.
ANALYZING

- What does the poet think of Charleston? *(doesn't like it; lists things he finds wrong)*
- What insects and animals does he single out? *(mosquitoes, centipedes,*

cockroaches, porpoises, sharks, alligators)

- Does Capt. Martin have anything good to say about Charleston? *(rum, hominy, and rice aren't "at a high price"; "large potatoes sweet as honey"; "many a bargain" for the right person who can "strike it")*
- Charleston was praised by others. Why do you think this poet has such a negative view of it? *(As the title says: it's "one men's view." Different people have different experiences and points of view.)*

North Carolina: Dissenters and Pirates

North Carolina emerged as a rather raucous, even rebellious colony. The most democratic of all colonies, it attracted free-spirited farmers, religious dissenters—and pirates.

ASK

1. Why did pirates choose the North Carolina coast for their hideouts? *(People in North Carolina minded their own business and left the pirates alone.)*
2. What did Blackbeard do to anger the governor? *(He blockaded an area off the North Carolina coast and made ships pay a bribe to pass through.)*
3. Why did colonists dislike the Navigation Acts? *(They didn't want to pay a tax to England on sales that took place between colonies.)*
4. What do you think is the "future event" Joy Hakim refers to in the last paragraph? *(the American Revolution)*

 **Ponder**
Why did archaeologists want to locate Blackbeard's ship?

✓ **Question Chart**

DISCUSS

1. How did people in North Carolina show their dislike of the Navigation Acts? *(refused to pay a tax on goods sold to other colonies; put British officials in jail; set up their own government under John Culpeper)*
2. Have students complete work on Resource 12 (TG page 87).

WRITE

Have students work with partners to write three questions they would like to ask Blackbeard, Mary Read, or Anne Bonney. Then students exchange papers. Imagining what these figures would say, they are to write answers to the questions their partners have posed.

LITERACY LINKS

Words to Discuss

treason	pirate
Navigation Acts	**bowsprit**

Link each of the words with at least one person or incident from the chapter. *(treason—John Culpeper; Navigation Acts—John Culpeper; pirate—Blackbeard; bowsprit—Blackbeard; Lt. Robert Maynard)*

Reading Skills
Evaluating Word Choice

Have students reread the chapter looking for the words and phrases Joy Hakim uses to paint a picture of Blackbeard. *(ferocious, braided his great black beard in pigtails, wove ribbons into them, hung smoking pieces of rope from his hat, coiling snakes, eerie look)* Ask: Why do you think the author wants readers to know how Blackbeard looked? *(to understand why people feared him and why he was a well-known pirate)*
VISUALIZING

Meeting Individual Needs
Visual Learners

Have students reread the Pieces of Eight feature on page 138. Visual learners can cut large circles of aluminum foil into eight equal pieces (to represent pieces of eight) and four small circles to represent quarters. Ask: If eight pieces of a *real* equaled one dollar, or 4 quarters, what would 4 pieces equal? *(2 quarters, or 50 cents)* Would you rather have two pieces of eight (two bits) or one quarter? *(They are worth the same.)*

THINKING ABOUT THE THEMES

The following questions will help students relate the book's themes to the content of Part 6. You may wish to use the questions for classroom discussion or have students answer them in written form.

1. What changes did tobacco bring about in Virginia? *(brought about more large plantations, more slaves; fewer small farmers; problems due to dependence on one-crop economy)*

2. Which Southern Colony was most diverse? Which was the least diverse? *(The Carolinas were most diverse; Virginia was least diverse.)*

3. How did slave laws attempt to stamp out anti-slavery efforts? *(Slave owners could not free their slaves; free black people could not own land.)*

4. Draw students' attention to the themes that have been posted around the room. Give them the opportunity to explore the relevance of these themes to Part 6. Accept choices that are supported by sound reasoning.

ASSESSING PART 6

Use Check-Up 6 (TG page 74) to assess student learning.

NOTE FROM JOY HAKIM

History challenges students in a way that is important for their mental development. It is a discipline that asks questions that can't always be answered. Consider, for example, a central paradox: How could we have had slavery in the land of the free? Mostly our books are terribly simplistic and moralistic on that. Slavery was evil. Period. Of course it was evil—but a lot of slave owners were not evil people. Thomas Jefferson and George Washington were not bad people. Why would they do something they knew was wrong? Children need information to wrestle with that thought. Do we do things we know are wrong? How will future generations judge us?

PROJECTS AND ACTIVITIES

▶ Charting Colonial Differences

Have teams of students create a chart with the following headings across the top: *Religious Tolerance, Political Rights, Economy, Slavery,* and *New England Colonies, Middle Colonies, Southern Colonies* down the side. Teams will fill in information about each group of colonies under each category.

▶ Graphing South Carolina's Slave Population

Have students study the graph and answer the questions on Resource 13 (TG page 88).

▶ Create a Dialogue

Ask students to imagine a conversation between Blackbeard and a member of the South Carolina or Virginia aristocracy. Have students work in pairs to write a dialogue between the two.

▶ Fact Sheet: The Thirteen English Colonies

Have students add information for the Southern Colonies on Resource 3 (TG page 78).

▶ Map of the English Colonies

Have students identify the colonies they have studied in Part 6 on Resource 9 (TG page 84).

▶ Timeline

Have students update their timelines with additional information from Part 6.

★ ★ FACTS TO SHARE ★ ★

In 1521 the Spanish explorer Francisco Gordillo led the first expedition to the Carolina coast. In 1526 a colony of 500 men, women, and children was established in what is now South Carolina. It failed because of bad weather and disease. Forty years later a French attempt to settle on the coast failed for lack of food.

The Colonies Continue Expanding

Expansion was a recurring theme throughout colonial American history. Expansion of land claims by colonists led to conflicts with Indians and eventually to the move westward. There was also expansion of trade and of ideas of individual freedom, even as colonists were enslaving more and more Africans.

SETTING GOALS

The goals for students in Part 7 are to:
- understand how the Glorious Revolution in England set the stage for greater democracy in America.
- examine the institution of slavery in America.
- understand the progression of settlement on the western frontier.
- investigate the impact on colonists of Daniel Boone and the Wilderness Road.

GETTING INTERESTED

1. Have students preview Chapters 37-42 by looking at titles, headings, illustrations, captions, margin notes, and quotations. Based on their review of these chapters, ask: In which directions do you think the colonies will expand? *(south and west)*

2. Create a class K-W-L chart related to the expansion of the American colonies. Have students contribute information for the categories, *What We Know; What We Want to Know; What We Have Learned*. Have students add to the chart as they read Chapters 37-42.

Working with Timelines
Direct students to the Chronology of Events on page 170. Have them look at the last eight entries to identify events they have not yet investigated *(1686, 1688, 1734, 1775)* and add these dates to their timelines.

Using Maps
Have students compare the map on Resource 2 (TG page 77) to the map on page 157. Discuss the different types of information available on each map. *(Resource 2—gives elevations and shows the extent of the Appalachian Mountains; page 157—shows area from Pennsylvania to North Carolina; shows ways to cross Appalachian Mountains)*

Royal Colonies and a No-Blood Revolution

In England's Glorious Revolution, James II lost his bid to become an absolute monarch and was deposed. Parliament, now more powerful than the monarchy, began exercising control over the colonies—much to the colonists' dismay.

ASK

1. What happened to James II and Andros when they tried to exert absolute power? *(Both were thrown out.)*
2. What is an absolute monarch? *(A ruler who has total power, unchecked by any other part of government.)*
3. According to a monarch, how does "divine right" give him or her the right to rule? *("Divine right" is the belief that God picked him or her for the job.)*

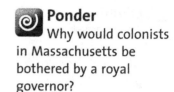 **Ponder**
Why would colonists in Massachusetts be bothered by a royal governor?

 **Question Chart**

DISCUSS

1. What is a revolution? *(an uprising of people against a government in which blood is shed and the ruler stripped of power and often executed)*
2. What is a no-blood revolution? *(change accomplished without any killing)*
3. What made colonists fear the loss of personal freedoms? *(They saw English actions toward the colonies as threats to the freedom they had gained when they left England.)*

WRITE

Have students imagine they are New England colonists who are angry at Sir Edmund Andros. Have them create a WANTED poster telling why they want him caught.

L I T E R A C Y   L I N K S

Words to Discuss

absolute monarch
divine right
Glorious Revolution

Have students use a dictionary and context to define the words and understand how they're connected. Point out that according to the Oxford English Dictionary, the Stuart kings were the first monarchs to use "divine right" to justify their rule.

Reading Skills
Understanding a Primary Source

Sourcebook: Introduce the English Bill of Rights (Source #8) by reading aloud the introduction. Then have students read these sections of the original document: paragraphs 4 *(levying money)*, 5 *(right of subjects to petition)*, 6 *(raising or keeping a standing army)*, 7 *(subjects which are protestants)*, and 10 *(excessive bail)*. Discuss why these particular rights were important to

people of the time and to people today. *(Students should understand that these rights limited the monarch's power. He could not tax anyone without Parliament's permission. No one could be punished for complaining to the monarch. He could not hire a peacetime army without Parliament's consent. The courts could not impose "excessive" bail or impose "cruel and unusual" punishments. The monarch's powers were severely reduced.)* CONNECTING

A Nasty Triangle

New England shippers developed triangular trade routes that linked New England with England, Africa, the West Indies, and other American Atlantic ports. Enslaved people were one of the major components of this trade, and they suffered unspeakably during these voyages.

ASK

1. Look at the map on page 145 and trace one of the triangles. How did the triangles of trade benefit the American colonies? What was the cost to Africans? *(benefit: trade with the rest of the world; cost to Africans: millions of people enslaved)*

2. In the triangular trade, what goods were sent from New England to England? *(lumber, cod, furs)* from the Southern Colonies to England *(indigo, rice, tobacco)* from England to Africa? *(guns, cloth)* from Africa to the West Indies? *(African people)* from the West Indies to New England? *(sugar, molasses)*

3. Why is an autobiography like Olaudah Equiano's so important? *(Few enslaved people were taught to read and write; therefore, there are not many written records of the experience of enslaved Africans.)*

⊙ Ponder
The English wouldn't let the colonists manufacture goods that competed with English goods. How did Americans feel about these restrictions?

☑ Question Chart

DISCUSS

1. What are the factors that opened up Africa to trade with Europe, the Caribbean, and America? *(Technology made it possible for European ships to reach Africa; Africans wanted European and American goods; Europeans and Americans wanted to sell slaves for profit.)*

2. What impressed you the most about Olaudah Equiano? *(Students most likely will be impressed with his ability to describe the events, to express his emotions, and to survive the experiences.)*

WRITE

Have students suppose that Olaudah is still alive. Ask them to write a letter to Olaudah, telling him their impressions of his autobiography.

LITERACY LINKS

Words to Discuss

triangular trade   slaver
commodity

Have students use a dictionary and context to define the words and understand the connections among them. Ask: Now that you know what *commodity* means, how do you think enslaved people felt when they were treated like commodities by slave traders?

Reading Skills
Understanding a Primary Source

Sourcebook: Read aloud the introduction to Source #7, the Resolution of the Germantown Quakers (1688). Have students read the first three lines of paragraph 1 *("These are the reasons . . . his life?")* and lines 11-18 *("There is a saying . . . we stand against.")* Ask: What are the Germantown Quakers' arguments against slavery? *(people who would not want to be slaves should not enslave others; based on the Golden Rule, slavery is wrong.)* ANALYZING

Skills Connection
Geography

Using details from the map on page 145 and the feature Africa, the Unknown Continent on pages 146-147, have students discuss why contact between Europe and Africa was difficult. *(The Sahara, the rough waters of the Atlantic, and the sheer size of Africa served as natural barriers to contact.)*

Four and Nine Make Thirteen

James Oglethorpe founded Georgia. The last of the 13 English colonies, Georgia was to be a haven for debtors who were imprisoned in England. The colonies fell into three groups—royal, self-governing, and proprietary.

ASK

1. Why did the Indians trust James Oglethorpe? *(He dealt with them honorably and always kept his word.)*
2. Which were the royal colonies? *(Virginia, Massachusetts, New Hampshire, New York, New Jersey, North Carolina, South Carolina, and Georgia)*
3. Which colonies governed themselves? *(Connecticut and Rhode Island)* Which were owned by individual "proprietors"? *(Pennsylvania and Maryland)*

◎ Ponder
How did the colonists' notion of the "frontier" conflict with the Indians' notion of the same land?

DISCUSS

1. Have students add information about Georgia to Resource 3 (TG page 78).
2. What was Oglethorpe's plan for the colony? *(to give debtors imprisoned in England a new start on small farms; to outlaw liquor and slavery)*
3. Where was the frontier and why would colonists in the mid-18th century be attracted to it? *(The frontier was land that was west of the Appalachian Mountains; in a farming society, owning land made people feel really free.)*

✔ Question Chart

WRITE

Have students write a paragraph describing Oglethorpe's "noble, inspiring" plan for Georgia—and why his plan didn't work out.

L I T E R A C Y   L I N K S

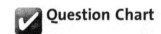

Words to Discuss

| proprietary colony | debtor |
| royal colony | frontier |

Have students use a dictionary and context to define the words and to understand the connections among them. Explain that *frontier* comes from the Latin *frons* ("front"). Ask: Do you like to be in the front of a line? Do you enjoy being the first to try new things?

Reading Skills
Evaluating Word Choice

Have students reread page 151, from paragraph 4, looking for words and phrases used to describe people who could succeed on the frontier. *(independent, equal, having intelligence, having strength, could be depended upon, tells the truth, can shoot straight, brave)* Ask: Who probably would not succeed on the frontier? *(people who cared about European class society; people who didn't like hard work)* INFERRING

Skills Connection
Geography

Have students locate Georgia on the map of the United States on page 182. Ask: What Spanish colony bordered Georgia in the mid-18th century? *(Florida)* Why was this a problem? *(Spain claimed Georgia and the Carolinas; the English in Georgia fought them off.)*

Over the Mountains

Extending from Quebec to Alabama, the Appalachian Mountains presented a formidable barrier to western migration. But tough people found a way across and settled the fertile valleys beyond the mountains.

ASK

1. What motivated colonists to travel over the mountains? *(trade with Indians, land, escape from problems)*

2. What were some of the problems frontiersmen and frontierswomen had to face? *(conflict with Indians, wild animals, backbreaking work)*

3. Why were log houses a good choice for frontier living? *(plenty of trees on the frontier; many had to be cut down in order to farm)*

⊚ **Ponder**
The trailblazers of the frontier faced unknown dangers and conditions. Would you have gone with them?

✓ **Question Chart**

DISCUSS

1. Use Resource 2 (TG page 77) to review the extent of the Appalachian Mountains described in the chapter. (Explain that the Adirondack Mountains in New York State are geologically part of the Canadian Shield, not the Appalachians.)

2. What do the Green Mountains, Blue Ridge, Catskill Mountains, and Great Smoky Mountains have in common? *(They are all part of the Appalachian mountain range.)*

3. Who was Talleyrand, and why is his account useful for understanding the frontier in the 18th century? *(A French prince and politician who traveled in the American west; few people wrote about the experience of moving west so his account helps us know what it was like.)*

WRITE

Ask students to imagine they traveled with Talleyrand on the part of his trip described on page 154. Have them write a diary entry describing their impression of their surroundings.

L I T E R A C Y   L I N K S

Words to Discuss

divide
pathfinder
frontiersman
frontierswoman
over-the-mountain people

Ask: Which word does not describe a person? *(divide)* Who were the first pathfinders in the eastern United States? *(Indians)* Which term describes a location? *(over-the-mountain)*

Reading Skills
Understanding Imagery

Have students reread the chapter, pointing out words and phrases that create images in their minds that help them understand what the frontier was like and what life was like for the trailblazers and first settlers west of the Appalachians. Have students make up their own images to describe life where they live. VISUALIZING

Meeting Individual Needs
Enrichment

Modern Americans can experience a semblance of the trailblazers' life on wilderness trails such as the Appalachian Trail, which follows the crest of the Appalachian Mountains from Georgia to Maine. Students may wish to visit the Appalachian Trail Conference Website at **www.appalachiantrail.org** to see pictures of the trail and read about its history.

Westward Ho

Parliament tried to stop westward expansion, but land-hungry colonists headed west anyway. Frontiersmen and frontierswomen risked everything for adventure or the dream of a better life. One of them was Daniel Boone.

ASK

1. Who was Daniel Boone? *(the most famous American frontiersman)*
2. What did John Finley, the fur trader, tell Daniel Boone about "kentake"? *(a beautiful meadowland, a hunting ground of the Indians full of birds, buffalo, deer, and beaver)*
3. What future state would be named for the place John Finley called "kentake"? *(Kentucky)*

DISCUSS

1. Why did the British try to stop colonists from moving west of the Appalachians? *(The British did not want to pay the cost of defending colonists from Indians or for governing new lands.)*
2. Why did colonists keep pushing west? *(Some were explorers, some were restless, some were looking for a good life.)*
3. Why did Indians want to keep white settlers from crossing through the Cumberland Gap? *(They wanted to keep their hunting grounds unspoiled.)*

⊙ Ponder
Frontier settlers learned from the Indians. What can happen when people show that they are willing to learn from one another?

✓ Question Chart

WRITE

Tell students they are filmmakers who are about to make a movie of Daniel Boone's life. Have them write a plan for a scene they want to film. They should include a description of the landscape and a summary of the action that will take place in the scene.

LITERACY LINKS

Words to Discuss

Wilderness Road
wilderness

Have students use a dictionary and context to define the words. Have them describe what conditions they would find on a "wilderness road."

Reading Skills
Interpreting Graphic Aids

Use the map on page 157 to help students understand elements of maps. Elicit the following information about map details. VISUALIZING

- What color is used for water? *(blue)* What bodies of water do you see? *(Ohio River, Atlantic Ocean, Chesapeake Bay)*
- What symbols are used for wilderness routes? *(red dots and dashes)* Name

the routes displayed. *(Great Trading Path, Boone's Trail, Wilderness Road, Warriors Path)* What symbols are used for mountains? *(triangle shapes)* Name the mountain chain shown. *(Appalachian Mountains)*

- Notice the different typestyles used. What kinds of letters are used to identify cities? *(script, capital and small letters)* wilderness routes? *(block capital letters)*

The End—and the Beginning

As this book ends, readers are invited to look ahead to the making of a nation out of 13 very different colonies.

ASK

1. Why did many of the people who came to America think they had found a "paradise"? *(They had more opportunities here than in the Old World; there was lots of land, fertile soil, many animals to hunt.)*

2. Many people dreamed of a free society. What did that mean? *(that people would be treated fairly)*

3. The title of this chapter is "The End—and the Beginning." The end of what? The beginning of what? *(the end of the book; the beginning of the colonies' struggle to become a free nation)*

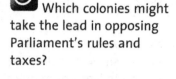

Ponder
Which colonies might take the lead in opposing Parliament's rules and taxes?

Question Chart

DISCUSS

1. Look at the portrait of George Washington on page 159. How would you describe the expression on his face? *(Responses may include intelligent, focused on the future, serious)*

2. Explain what the caption under the picture means by "extraordinary career." *(general who defeated the British in the American Revolution; first President of the United States)*

WRITE

Tell students to imagine they are sending a postcard to England in the mid-18th century from one of the colonies. On one side of the postcard is the illustration opposite the copyright page in their book. For the other side of the card, they are to write a note describing their new colonial home, telling how the illustration does or does not show a true picture of where they have settled.

LITERACY LINKS

Words to Discuss

Read the quotation in the fourth paragraph; "conceived in liberty and dedicated to the proposition that all men are created equal." Explain that these words are in the first sentence of Lincoln's Gettysburg Address. In it he was reminding people of what our country (then fighting a bitter Civil War) stands for. Ask: Why do you think Joy Hakim uses those words in this chapter? *(to give a taste of where the story is leading)*

Reading Skills
Evaluating Word Choice

Have students reread Chapter 42 and identify the places where Joy Hakim makes a promise to readers through her choice of words. Pose these questions. CONNECTING

- In the last two paragraphs of the chapter, what examples can you find of the author's use of the future tense? *(The dreamers will . . . ; They will . . . ; you will learn . . . meet . . . learn; the story will. . . .)*

- Why do you think she has chosen to use the future tense in these paragraphs? *(to interest readers in what comes next; to increase anticipation; to make a promise to the reader)*

A Cartographer Makes Maps, Not Wagons

Mapmakers were among the most important people of the 16th and 17th centuries. Without accurate maps, explorers could not reliably find their way around the world. Gerhardus Mercator and Father Vincenzo Coronelli became famous for making the best maps in Europe.

ASK

1. What maps do you use? On a Website, what is a site map? How does it differ from a road map? *(Responses will vary.)*
2. Why did Portuguese sailors treat their maps like secret documents? *(to give Portugal an advantage over other countries in trading and exploring)*
3. Why would mapmakers put their country in the center of a map? *(because they felt that their country should be the most important feature of the map)*

⊚ Ponder
What do people come to believe when they always see their country in the center of world maps?

DISCUSS

1. What did Mercator do that no mapmaker had done before? *(He developed a projection of the globe—a two-dimensional map from a sphere—that allowed him to draw straight lines of latitude and longitude.)*
2. What advantage did Father Coronelli have over other mapmakers? *(He received information about the world from many different countries, so his maps were more detailed and accurate than those of other mapmakers.)*
3. Use Resource 14 (TG page 89) to help students understand latitude and longitude. Encourage students to use wall maps in the classroom to challenge other students to identify places when given their latitude and longitude.

☑ Question Chart

WRITE

Ask students to suppose it is the 17th century. Have them write a letter to Father Coronelli inviting him to come see North America for himself. They should be sure to comment on his maps!

LITERACY LINKS

Words to Discuss

atlas   longitude
globe   latitude
cartography

Have students use a dictionary and context to define the words and understand the connections among them. Ask: which of these words was known to Father Coronelli? *(all of them)* Have students choose one of the first three words and explain its relation to Coronelli and to satellite photography.

Reading Skills
Comparing Maps

Have students look at the two maps of the Great Lakes on page 164 and read the caption. Ask: What does Joy Hakim mean when she writes: "Amazing, isn't it?" *(Coronelli, who had never seen the Great Lakes, came so close to being accurate—and he did it over 300 years ago!)* In what way are the maps very similar? *(their shapes)* What does the satellite photograph show that Coronelli's map doesn't? *(There's more distance between Lake Erie and Lake Ontario; Lake Michigan is longer; Lake Huron branches out somewhat.)*
CONNECTING

Meeting Individual Needs
Reteaching

Have students use the Measuring Words feature on page 167 to make flash cards, with the terms on one side and a definition or description on the back. They can use the cards to study or to quiz each other.

THINKING ABOUT THE THEMES

The following questions will help students relate the book's themes to the content of Part 7. You may wish to use the questions for classroom discussion or have students answer them in written form.

1. Use Resource 10 (TG page 85) to compare the growth of selected colonies' populations between 1670 and 1740. How will these increases affect the diversity of the population? *(More people means greater diversity; people will bring their ideas, talent, and cultures to mix with those already here.)*

2. What conflicts do you think will develop as settlers move west across the Appalachians? *(conflicts between settlers and the British rulers who forbid colonists to move west; conflicts with Indians)*

3. Draw students' attention to the themes that have been posted around the room. Give them the opportunity to explore the relevance of these themes to Part 7. Accept choices that are supported by sound reasoning.

ASSESSING PART 7

Use Check-Up 7 (TG page 75) to assess student learning.

NOTE FROM JOY HAKIM

I like to ask students to write their own tests. They have to think to do that. Then I have them answer their own questions and someone else's as well.

 FACTS TO SHARE

Even as an old man Daniel Boone was on the move west, heading out toward the Mississippi. The story goes that along the way other settlers would recognize him and shout, "Where you headed to, Daniel? Why are you leaving?" And Boone would reply, "Headin' west. Too crowded here. I want more elbow room."

PROJECTS AND ACTIVITIES

 Thirteen Clues for Thirteen Colonies

Have students answer the questions on Resource 15 (TG page 90). Then ask each student to make up a clue and collect them for a new class challenge.

K-W-L Chart

Have students complete the K-W-L chart they started at the beginning of Part 7.

Debate Westward Expansion

Provide the class with this proposition, *Resolved:* Britain was right to prohibit settlement west of the Appalachians. Have students prepare arguments, pro and con. *(Pro: settlers had pushed Indians off their lands along the Atlantic coast; the territory west of the mountains should be left to them. Con: a growing population required more land so new deals should be made with the Indians.)*

Class Almanac: Prediction

Ask: In Part 7, what signs of trouble between England and its American colonies do you see? *(Parliament's takeover of Massachusetts and Parliament's banning of western settlement violates what colonists' see as their rights; it could lead to resistance.)* Now have them add a prediction to their Class Almanac (Part 5).

Map of the English Colonies

Have students add Georgia and complete the map on Resource 9 (TG page 84).

Using the Timeline

When students have updated their timelines with additional information from Part 7, have them work with a partner to pick the "milestones of colonial America." You can assign half the class milestones related to religious freedom. *(Roger Williams founds Providence, Anne Hutchinson is banished from Massachusetts, the proprietors' charter for New York and New Jersey, William Penn founds Pennsylvania)* Assign the other half milestones related to representative government. *(Mayflower Compact, representative Court of Massachusetts, House of Burgesses, Penn's Charter of Liberties, overthrow of Andros in Massachusetts)*

Name _____ Date _____

Check-Up 1

Answering these questions will help you understand and remember what you have read in Chapters 1-6. Write your answers on a separate sheet of paper.

1. These people played key roles in the events described in Chapters 1-6. Tell who each person was and how he or she made a difference.
   a. Galileo
   b. Christopher Newport
   c. Powhatan
   d. John Smith
   e. Pocahontas

2. How did the Powhatans make use of the land?

3. What did the first Jamestown settlers expect to find in Virginia?

4. Why was Jamestown such a poor place for a settlement?

5. Define each of these terms. Then explain its importance for Jamestown.
   a. London Company
   b. younkers
   c. yeoman
   d. Starving Time

6. Why were the first settlers in Jamestown so unprepared?

7. How did Powhatan help the Jamestown settlers? How did he harm them?

8. In October 1609, John Smith left Jamestown, never to return. What happened to him?

9. What changes will the English settlers have to make to succeed at Jamestown?

10. Use the map to answer these questions.
    a. Why did the English settlers choose this location for Jamestown?
    b. Why did this location become a trap in the Starving Time?

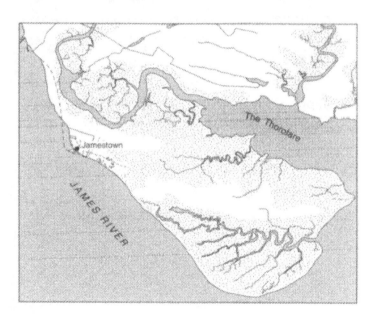

Name _____   Date _____

Check-Up 2

Answering these questions will help you understand and remember what you have read in Chapters 7-12. Write your answers on a separate sheet of paper.

1. These pairs of people are important to the events in Chapters 7-12. How are the people in each pair connected? What role did each person play in Virginia?
   a. Lord de la Warr, Sir Thomas Dale
   b. Pocahontas, John Rolfe
   c. Opechancanough, Chanco

2. How did a hurricane nearly spell the end for Jamestown?

3. Define each term. Then explain its significance to people in the colony of Virginia.
   a. indentured servants
   b. House of Burgesses
   c. tobacco

4. Write a paragraph contrasting Pocahontas's childhood with her adult life.

5. Why didn't King James approve of tobacco?

6. How did slavery take hold in Virginia?

7. What about slavery contradicts the idea of freedom?

8. Why was 1619 a big year for Virginia?

9. European kings and queens believed they had "divine right." What did that mean?

10. Indicate the year of these important events at Jamestown on the timeline. Label the timeline with the corresponding letters.
    a. House of Burgesses is formed.
    b. Great Massacre occurs.
    c. Lord de la Warr arrives.

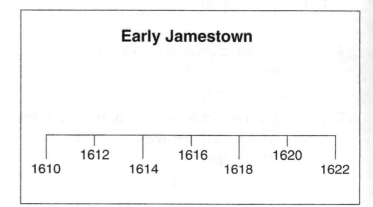

Early Jamestown

| 1610 | 1612 | 1614 | 1616 | 1618 | 1620 | 1622 |

Name _____ Date _____

Check-Up 3

Answering these questions will help you understand and remember what you have
read in Chapters 13-16. Write your answers on a separate sheet of paper.

1. These people played key roles in founding
   Massachusetts. Tell who each person was and
   what he did to help the colony.
   a. William Bradford
   b. Massasoit
   c. Samoset
   d. Squanto
   e. John Winthrop

2. Describe the significance of each of the
   following places in the founding of
   Massachusetts.
   a. Leyden, Holland
   b. Plymouth, Massachusetts
   c. Massachusetts Bay Colony

3. Define each of these terms. Then explain why
   it was important to the events of the time.
   a. established church
   b. Mayflower Compact
   c. toleration
   d. General Court

4. The opinions of the Pilgrims and the Puritans
   about the Anglican Church differed. What was
   the difference?

5. Define each of these forms of government.
   a. representative democracy
   b. direct democracy
   c. autocracy
   d. aristocracy

6. Why did Puritans believe that children should
   be taught to read?

7. Was the government of the Massachusetts
   Bay Colony a theocracy? Explain why or why
   not.

8. Imagine you are a young person living in a
   village in colonial New England. What do you
   like best about living there? What do you like
   least? Explain your reasons.

9. Will the religious intolerance of the Puritans
   cause trouble in the Massachusetts Bay
   Colony? Explain why or why not.

10. The Pilgrims and the Puritans were closely
    related, but there were differences between
    them. Use the Venn diagram to show which
    ideas refer to the Pilgrims, which to the
    Puritans, and which to both. Label the
    diagram with the corresponding letters.
    a. outlaw the Catholic Church
    b. purify the Church of England
    c. separate from the Church of England
    d. people could speak directly to God
    e. did not have religious freedom in England
    f. did not tolerate other religions

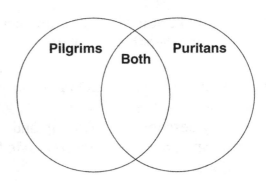

Name _____   Date _____

Check-Up 4

Answering these questions will help you understand and remember what you have read in Chapters 17-23. Write your answers on a separate sheet of paper.

1. These people played key roles in the events described in Chapters 17-23. Tell what each one did that was important in this period.
   a. Roger Williams
   b. Anne Hutchinson
   c. Samuel Sewall
   d. Metacom-Philip
   e. Popé

2. Why did New England colonists settle in the Connecticut River Valley?

3. Both Puritans and Quakers had strong beliefs about these ideas. Define each term. Then tell if the Quakers and Puritans were for or against it.
   a. freedom of conscience
   b. oath of allegiance
   c. divine right of kings

4. Define these terms. Then explain how each one relates to the New England colonies.
   a. gallows
   b. chattel
   c. banished

5. Quakers and Puritans had different views about women. What were they?

6. Imagine you are a young person in Salem during and after the witchcraft trials. Write a diary entry describing how gossip and suspicion spread until no one was safe from accusations.

7. These events were important to the relationship between Indians and settlers in 17th-century America. Tell what happened in each.
   a. Pequot War
   b. King Philip's War
   c. Pueblo Uprising

8. The Indians and the settlers had different views about land. What were these differences?

9. The Pueblo and Wampanoag Indians had different experiences with Europeans. Contrast their experiences.

10. This map shows the New England Colonies in 1650. Label the map with the letters corresponding to the people who founded each colony.
    a. Puritans from England
    b. Pilgrims from England
    c. Roger Williams and his followers
    d. Thomas Hooker and his followers
    e. Puritans from Massachusetts
    f. John Mason
    g. Ferdinando Gorges

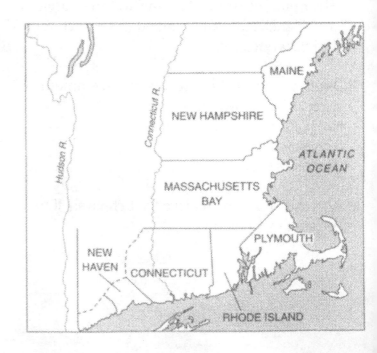

Name _____ Date _____

Check-Up 5

Answering these questions will help you understand and remember what you have
read in Chapters 24-29. Write your answers on a separate sheet of paper.

1. These people played key roles in the founding
   of the Middle Colonies. Tell who each person
   was and what role he played.
   a. Peter Stuyvesant
   b. Johan Printz
   c. Sir George Carteret
   d. Lord John Berkeley
   e. William Penn

2. List these colonies in the order in which they
   were founded: New York, New Netherland,
   New Jersey.

3. Give details about each of these terms. Then
   explain its significance to the events of the
   time.
   a. fur trade
   b. patroon
   c. proprietor

4. Write a paragraph explaining who these
   people are and their importance to the
   English Civil War.
   a. Oliver Cromwell
   b. King Charles I
   c. Cavaliers
   d. Roundheads

5. In what ways did the reign of King Charles II
   encourage English colonization in America?

6. What did the charter for New York and New
   Jersey have in common with William Penn's
   Charter of Liberties?

7. In what ways did William Penn stand for
   Quaker ideals?

8. What qualities do you think Benjamin
   Franklin had that made it possible for him to
   accomplish so much?

9. The Middle Colonies had a great diversity of
   people and religions. How did that lead to
   change?

10. This map shows the Middle Colonies in 1685.
    Label the map with the letters corresponding
    to the names of the colonies.
    a. East Jersey
    b. West Jersey
    c. Pennsylvania
    d. New York
    e. Three Lower Counties (Delaware)

Name _____   Date _____

Check-Up 6

Answering these questions will help you understand and remember what you have read in Chapters 30-36. Write your answers on a separate sheet of paper.

1. These people played key roles in the events described in Chapters 30-36. Tell what each person or persons did.
   a. Calvert family
   b. John Culpeper
   c. Blackbeard, Mary Read, Anne Bonney

2. How did agriculture affect the growth of the Southern Colonies?

3. How was each of the following acts significant in colonial development?
   a. Toleration Act
   b. Indian Act of 1714
   c. Navigation Acts

4. Define each of the following terms:
   a. apprentice
   b. indigo
   c. Gullah

5. What would be a typical day for one of these people? Write a diary entry or daily schedule for the person you choose.
   a. child of a plantation owner
   b. child of a yeoman farmer
   c. young indentured servant
   d. young slave

6. List these colonies from greatest religious tolerance to least religious tolerance: Maryland, Virginia, North Carolina.

7. Imagine you are in Williamsburg for a House of Burgesses meeting. Name a delegate you would like to meet. What is one question you would ask him?

8. List some of the features that made the Southern Colonies different from the New England and Middle Colonies.

9. In 1677, why did some North Carolinians rebel against England?

10. This map shows the Southern Colonies. Match each fact with its colony by labeling the map with the corresponding letters.
    a. This colony had the busiest port in the Southern Colonies.
    b. The coast of this colony was a hideout for pirates.
    c. This colony's capital rang with debates about government in America.
    d. This colony practiced religious tolerance for Christians.

Name _____   Date _____

Check-Up 7

Answering these questions will help you understand and remember what you have read in Chapters 37-42. Write your answers on a separate sheet of paper.

1. These people played key roles in the events described in Chapters 37-42. Tell who each person was and what he did of importance in this period.
   a. King James II
   b. Olaudah Equiano
   c. James Oglethorpe
   d. Daniel Boone

2. Explain how the Appalachian Mountains affected settlers who wanted to move west.

3. Define each of these terms. Then explain why it was important to the geography of colonial America.
   a. divide
   b. gap
   c. Wilderness Road

4. Describe how each of these kinds of colonies was governed.
   a. royal
   b. proprietary
   c. self-governing

5. How do you think England's Glorious Revolution influenced the colonists?

6. Which was the last of the thirteen English colonies to be settled?

7. By the mid-1700s, why did many settlers want to move west?

8. Pick one of the thirteen colonies and explain why you would have liked to live there.

9. Write one paragraph explaining the English government's ideas about settlement of western lands. Write a second paragraph explaining American colonists' ideas about the subject.

10. Complete the chart by checking the type of government that applies to each of the 13 English colonies in 1752.

Colony	Royal	Self-Governing	Proprietary
New Hampshire			
Massachusetts			
Rhode Island			
Connecticut			
New York			
New Jersey			
Pennsylvania			
Maryland			
Delaware			
Virginia			
North Carolina			
South Carolina			
Georgia			

Name _____ Date _____

Resource 1

QUESTION CHART: *MAKING THIRTEEN COLONIES*

★ What were the major events?

_____   _____
_____   _____
_____   _____
_____   _____
_____   _____
_____   _____

★ Who were the significant people?

_____   _____
_____   _____
_____   _____
_____   _____
_____   _____
_____   _____

★ What were the important ideas?

_____
_____
_____
_____
_____
_____
_____
_____

Name _____ Date _____

Resource 2

ELEVATION MAP OF THE EASTERN UNITED STATES

Directions An elevation map tells you how high above sea level a place is. The symbols in the map key tell you the general elevation of places on the map. On the map, most of Michigan (MI) is covered by a light gray color with diagonal lines. That means the land is between 650 and 1,599 feet above sea level. Use the map to answer the questions below.

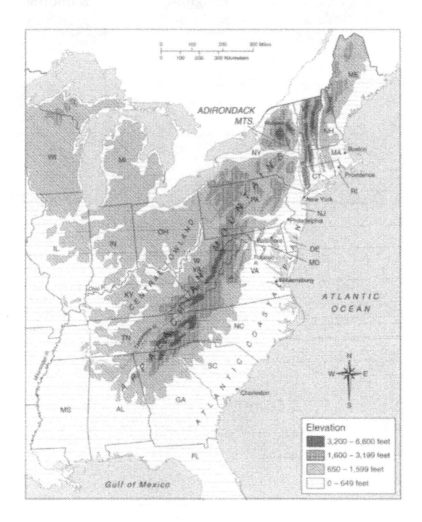

1. What mountain ranges are shown on the map? What are the highest elevations?

_____

2. The best farming is in low, flat regions. Using the map, explain why farming was so important to the economy of the Southern Colonies.

_____

3. Using the map, explain why traveling westward during colonial times was so difficult.

_____

Resource 3

FACT SHEET: THE 13 ENGLISH COLONIES

Directions   As you read, use this chart to help you organize facts about each colony. (Some information has been filled in.) You can also add facts from the Resources map on page 185.

Colony (Founded)	Founders	Religious Attitude	Economic Activities	Government/ Charter
Virginia (1607)				
Massachusetts (1620)				
Rhode Island (1636)				
Connecticut (1636)	Thomas Hooker	tolerant	farming	self-governing; Fundamental Orders
New Hampshire (1630)				
New York (1664)				
Delaware (1664)				
New Jersey (1660)				
Pennsylvania (1681)				
Maryland (1634)				
South Carolina (1670)				
North Carolina (1712)				
Georgia (1732)				

Resource 4

WHAT JOHN SMITH AND THE POWHATAN SAID

Directions   **Read each quotation. Then write a sentence or two explaining what the statement reveals about the relationship between the English and Powhatans in Virginia.**

1. "With sixteen bushels of Corn [received in trade with Indians] I returned towards our Fort: by the way I encountered with two Canoes of Indians. . . . [They] requested me to return to their Town, where I should load my boat with corn: and with near thirty bushels I returned to the fort."—*John Smith*

_____

_____

_____

2. ". . . many do inform me, your coming is not for trade, but to invade my people and possess my Country."—*Wahunsonacock, the Powhatan*

_____

_____

_____

3. "Some ten years ago being in Virginia, and taken prisoner by the power of Powhatan their chief King, I received from this great savage exceeding great courtesy."—*John Smith*

_____

_____

_____

4. "Why will you take by force what you may have quietly by love? Why will you destroy us who supply you with food? What can you get by war?"—*Wahunsonacock, the Powhatan*

_____

_____

_____

Name _____ Date _____

Resource 5

WHAT VIRGINIA SETTLERS NEEDED

Directions This pamphlet was published in London in 1622 by Felix Kyngston. It was for people thinking of settling in Virginia. Included were lists of items settlers needed. Review these lists. Then answer the questions on a separate sheet of paper.

Introduction
The Inconveniences that have happened to some persons which have transported themselves from England to Virginia, without provisions necessary to sustain themselves, has greatly hindered the progress of the noble plantation [colony].

Apparel
For one man:
One cap
Three shirts
One waistcoat
One suit of cloth
Three pair of stockings
Four pair of shoes

Victuals
For a whole year for one man:
Eight bushels of meal
Two bushels of [dried] peas
Two bushels of oatmeal
One gallon of oil
Two gallons of vinegar

Arms
For one man:
One armor complete (light)
One long piece [musket], five feet or five and a half
One sword
One belt
Twenty pounds of powder
Sixty pounds of shot or lead, pistol and
    goose shot

Tools
For a family of 6 persons:
Five broad hoes
Five narrow hoes
Two broad axes
Five felling axes
Two steel hand saws
Two two-hand saws
Two hammers
Three shovels
Two spades
Two augers
Six chisels
One grindstone
Nails of all sorts
Two pickaxes

Household Implements
One iron pot
One kettle
One large frying pan
Two skillets
One spit [metal rod for holding and turning meat over fire]
Platters, dishes, spoons of wood

For One Man
Estimated cost of passage to Virginia: 6 pounds
Estimated cost of transporting provisions: 1 pound

1. What had happened in Virginia before 1622 that made this pamphlet necessary?

2. Is there an item that surprises you? Is anything missing from the list that you would want to know about?

3. Based on what you know about Virginia, which item on the list may be more trouble than it's worth?

4. What conclusions can you draw from the number of tools needed for a "family of 6 persons"?

Name _____   Date _____

Resource 6

COMPARING MAPS: INDIAN LANDS IN NEW ENGLAND, 1674 AND 1774

Directions   Compare the two maps. Then answer the questions.

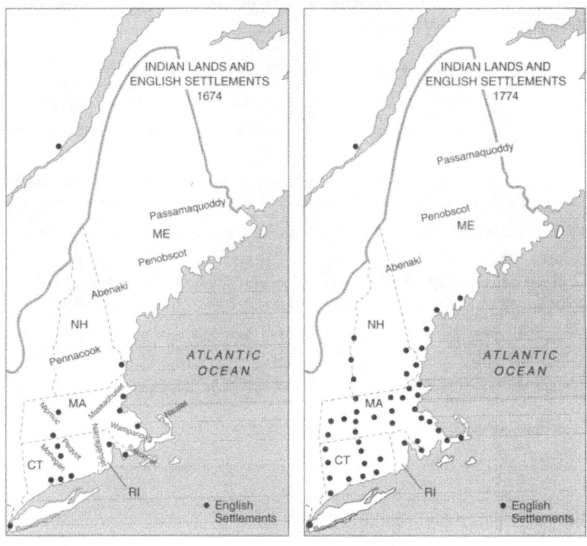

1. What conclusions can you draw from the 1674 map about possible conflicts between Indians and colonists?

_____

_____

2. What changed for the New England Indians between 1674 and 1774?

_____

_____

3. Why do you think the Indians were able to keep their lands in Maine in 1774?

_____

_____

Resource 7

A TREATY OF PEACE

Directions   The following is an account of the 1621 treaty between the Pilgrims and Massasoit (chief of the Wampanoags). (No copy of the actual treaty exists; this account was written down later.) Read the account. Then answer the questions below.

Then they treated of peace, which was:

1. That neither he [Massasoit] nor any of his should injure or do hurt to any of our people.

2. And if any of his did hurt to any of ours, he should send the offender, that we might punish him.

3. That if any of our tools were taken away when our people are at work, he should cause them to be restored, and if ours did any harm to any of his, we would do the likewise to them.

4. If any did unjustly war against him, we would aid him; if any did war against us, he should aid us.

5. He should send to his neighbor confederates [friendly tribes], to certify them of this, that they might not wrong us, but might be likewise comprised in the conditions of peace.

6. That when their men came to us, they should leave their bows and arrows behind them, as we should do our pieces when we came to them.

Lastly, that doing thus, King James would esteem of him as his friend and ally.

1. What do paragraphs 1–3 discuss?

_____

_____

2. What does paragraph 4 require both sides to do?

_____

_____

3. How would paragraph 6 help relations between the two sides?

_____

_____

4. The agreement does not discuss use of the land. How might that cause future problems?

_____

_____

Resource 8

MARY ROWLANDSON, CAPTIVE

In February 1676, during King Philip's War, Indians attacked Lancaster, Massachusetts. They took Mary Rowlandson and her three children captive. Her older son and daughter were separated from her. Her wounded six-year-old daughter stayed with her but died after nine days. For three months the Indians kept the grieving Rowlandson with them as they wandered through the New England forests. Her narrative was published in 1682, six years after she was reunited with her husband and two surviving children.

Directions   **Read the excerpts from Mary Rowlandson's story. Then, on a separate sheet of paper, write one or two paragraphs summarizing Rowlandson's experience.**

The Attack On the tenth of February 1676, came the Indians with great numbers upon Lancaster: their first coming was about sunrising; hearing the noise of some guns, we looked out; several houses were burning. . . . I took my children . . . to go forth and leave the house: but as soon as we came to the door and appeared, the Indians shot so thick that the bullets rattled against the house, as if one had taken an handful of stones and threw them. . . . The Indians laid hold of us, pulling me one way, and the children another, and said . . . if I were willing to go along with them, they would not hurt me.

Eating The first week of my being among them I hardly ate any thing; the second week I found my stomach grow very faint for want of something; and yet it was very hard to get down their filthy trash; but the third week, though I could think how formerly my stomach would turn against this or that, and I could starve and die before I could eat such things, yet they were sweet and savory to my taste. . . .

Meeting King Philip I went to see King Philip. He bade me come in and sit down, and asked me whether I would smoke . . . (a usual compliment . . .) but this no way suited me. . . . During my abode in this place, Philip spake to me to make a shirt for his boy, which I did. . . . Afterwards he asked me to make a cap for his boy, for which he invited me to dinner. I went, and he gave me a pancake . . . made of parched wheat, beaten, and fried in bear's grease, but I thought I never tasted pleasanter meat in my life. . . .

A Kindness One bitter cold day I could find no room to sit down before the fire. I went out, and could not tell what to do, but I went in to another wigwam, where they were also sitting round the fire, but the squaw laid a skin for me, and bid me sit down, and gave me some ground nuts, and bade me come again . . . and yet these were strangers to me that I never saw before. . . .

Indian Survival It was thought [by the English settlers], if [the Indians'] corn were cut down, they would starve and die with hunger, and all their corn that could be found, was destroyed, and they driven from that little they had in store, into the woods in the midst of winter; and yet . . . I did not see (all the time I was among them) one man, woman, or child, die with hunger. . . . The chief and commonest food was ground nuts. They eat also nuts and acorns . . . and several other weeds and roots, that I know not. . . . They would eat horse's guts, and ears, and all sorts of wild birds . . . also bear, venison, beaver, tortoise, frogs, squirrels, dogs, skunks, rattlesnakes; yea, the very bark of trees. . . . I can but stand in admiration to see the wonderful power of God in providing for such a vast number of our enemies in the wilderness, where there was nothing to be seen, but from hand to mouth.

Resource 9

MAPPING THE 13 ENGLISH COLONIES

Directions   On the map, label each colony with its correct name. Then color the New England Colonies blue, the Middle Colonies red, and the Southern Colonies green.

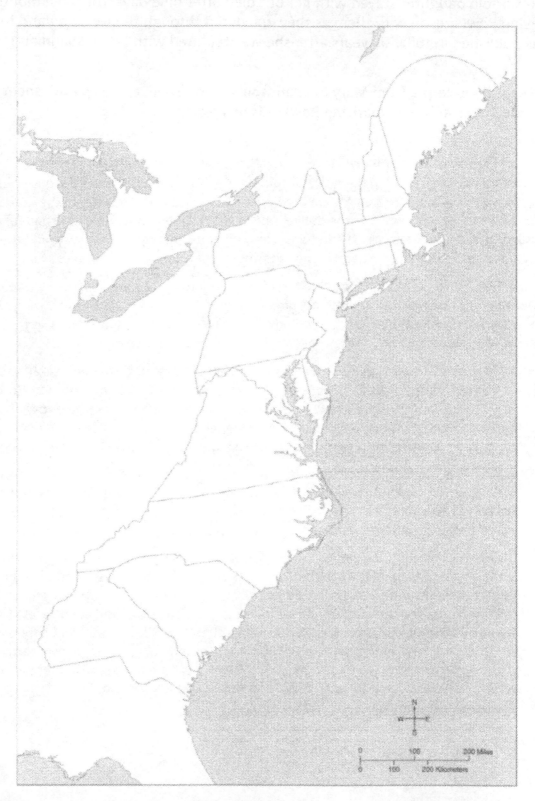

Resource 10

POPULATION OF SELECTED COLONIES, 1670-1740

Directions   Line graphs can help you trace changes in population over time. Read the graph. Then answer the questions.

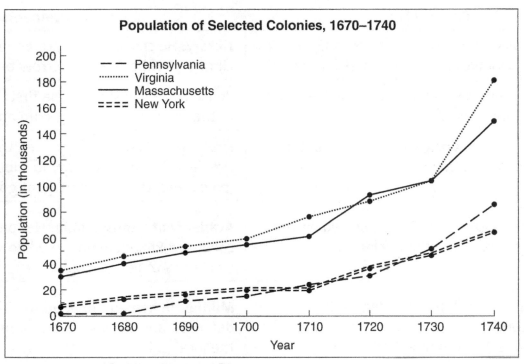

Source: *Historical Statistics of the United States.*
Colonial Times to 1970. U.S. Census Bureau

1. Which colony had the largest population in 1670? Approximately what was the population?

_____

2. In which year did Massachusetts and Virginia have approximately the same population? What was that population?

_____

3. Which colony had the largest population in 1740? What was the approximate number?

_____

4. What was the first year in which Pennsylvania's population was larger than New York's?

_____

Name _____   Date _____

Resource 11

BENJAMIN FRANKLIN: AMERICAN HERO

Directions   This chart lists some of the contributions Ben Franklin made to American political life and society. Read the chart and then answer the questions.

Political Life	Civic Improvements
Political Essays: From the time he was 12, he published his views about the American colonies.	**Library:** He created the first lending library. Library members could borrow books.
Political Cartoons: He created the first American political cartoon, called "Plain Truth."	**Police Force:** He started the first "town watch" in the colonies to prevent criminal activity.
Second Continental Congress: He represented Pennsylvania at the Congress.	**Fire Department:** He organized the first city fire department. People who subscribed (paid a fee) to the department got protection.
Declaration of Independence: He served on the committee that drafted the Declaration.	**Academy of Pennsylvania:** He founded a college in Philadelphia, now known as the University of Pennsylvania.
Constitution: He outlined the idea for two houses of Congress (Senate and House of Representatives), combining limited and direct representation.	**Militia:** He helped provided for "the common defense," and even served as a private in the local militia.
Ambassador to Europe: He was the first American to officially represent American interests in foreign countries.	**Environment:** He was a major force in cleaning up pollution along Philadelphia's waterfront.

1. Which contribution to political life do you think was the most important? Explain your answer.

_____

_____

_____

2. Which civic improvement do you think was the most important? Explain your answer.

_____

_____

_____

Name _____ Date _____

Resource 12

FREE AND SLAVE POPULATION IN SOUTH CAROLINA, 1700-1770

Numerical information about a topic can be expressed using several visual aids. Two of those visual aids are a *table* and a *bar graph*. A table presents exact numbers about a topic in an orderly fashion. A bar graph turns those numbers into a dramatic visual aid that makes it easy for the reader to understand the importance of the numbers.

Directions   Use the data in the table to make a bar graph. (The bars for 1700 have been done as an example.) You will need a ruler, a black pencil, and two different-colored pencils. Follow these steps.

1. Round each number to the nearest thousand.
2. Using the ruler, mark the height of each bar with the black pencil. There should be two bars for each year.
3. Using the ruler, draw the bars with the black pencil.
4. Use one colored pencil to fill in the Free Population bars; use the other colored pencil to fill in the Slave Population bars.
5. Use the colored pencils to complete the graph legend.

Free and Slave Population—South Carolina

Year	1700	1710	1720	1730	1740	1750	1760	1770
Free	3,260	6,783	5,048	10,000	15,000	25,000	36,740	49,066
Slave	2,444	4,100	12,000	20,000	30,000	39,000	57,334	75,718

Source: *Historical Statistics of the United States: Colonial Times to 1970.* U.S. Census Bureau.

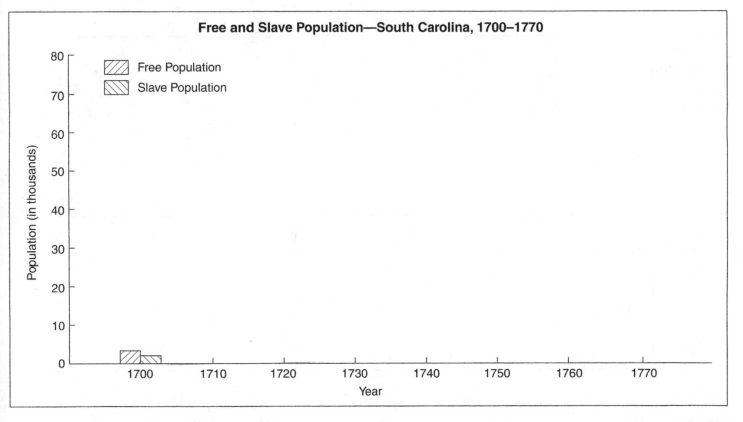

Name _____ Date _____

Resource 13

QUESTIONING THE CAROLINAS

Directions   North and South Carolina developed into two very different colonies. Use the information in Chapters 35 and 36 to complete this chart about the two colonies.

Question	South Carolina	North Carolina
1. Where did your settlers come from?		
2. What were the economic activities in your colony?		
3. Did you tolerate many religions?		
4. How democratic was your colonial government? (Give details.)		

Name _____   Date _____

Resource 14

USING LATITUDE AND LONGITUDE

Mapmakers use a grid system based on latitude and longitude to describe locations on the earth. The horizontal lines across the map below are **latitude.** All points on any line of latitude (called **parallels**) are the same number of degrees (°) north or south of the equator.

The vertical lines from top to bottom on the map are **longitude.** All points on any line of longitude (called **meridians**) are the same number of degrees (°) east or west of the Prime Meridian, which runs through Greenwich, England.

To tell where a point is on a map, you give the latitude and longitude of the spot. Find Trenton, New Jersey, on the map. It is where the parallel 40°N meets the meridian 75°W. We say that Trenton is at 40°N 75°W.

Directions   **Use the map to find the approximate latitude and longitude of these cities.**

1. Washington, DC _____

2. Santa Fe, NM _____

3. Albany, NY _____

4. Sacramento, CA _____

5. Austin, TX _____

6. Bismarck, ND _____

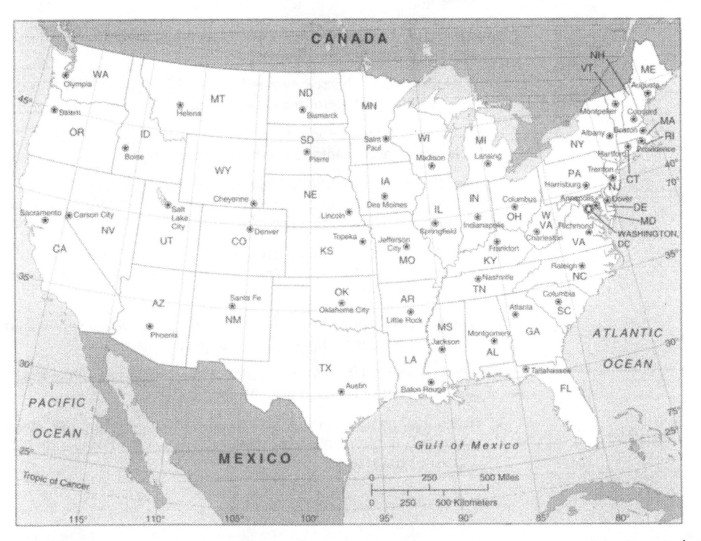

Resource 15

THIRTEEN CLUES FOR THIRTEEN COLONIES

Directions   Write the name of the colony that matches each clue in the space next to the number.

_____ 1. *Think "Big Tub"*—The Swedes and Dutch lost it; the English claimed it and named it.

_____ 2. *Oh, Oh, Oglethorpe!*—English debtors were supposed to settle here in a model colony, but farmers and tradesmen got the job.

_____ 3. *No, Not New York!*—This Dutch colony with a patroon farm system was taken over by the English king and given to two of his friends.

_____ 4. *"Providentially" the Narraganset Were Willing to Sell*—Founded by Roger Williams, who paid the Indians for it and treated them as equals, this colony welcomed people of different religions.

_____ 5. *Middle? Southern? What Are You?* This proprietary colony was owned by the Calverts. Catholics and other Christians were welcome; others were not.

_____ 6. *Heads Up!*—This colony was home to yeoman farmers, religious dissenters and the most famous pirate of all.

_____ 7. *Brotherly Love*—This colony was founded by a Quaker who treated Indians fairly and permitted religious equality for all.

_____ 8. *Starving No More*—Home to some of the first English settlers, this colony's tobacco plantations put it on the map.

_____ 9. *And I'll Throw in the White Mountains!*—Originally part of Massachusetts, the king gave it to a friend of his, George Mason, as a proprietary colony with its own charter.

_____ 10. *Are We There Yet?* Puritans left Massachusetts on foot and found fertile land in a river valley. They petitioned the crown for a charter to start this colony.

_____ 11. *The Rice and Indigo Blues*—Planters from the Caribbean settled here to make fortunes raising rice and indigo with slave labor.

_____ 12. *Quakers and Witches Not Allowed!*—Home to Pilgrims and Puritans, this colony once included present-day Maine.

_____ 13. *The Bargain of the Century?* This colony was bought from the Indians and run by iron-fisted, silver-nailed Peter Stuyvesant before the English showed up.

ANSWER KEY

CHECK-UP 1

1. (a) showed that the sun, not the earth, was the center of the universe (b) captain of ship bringing settlers to Jamestown in 1607 (c) chief of the Powhatans who both helped and fought Jamestown settlers (d) became leader of Jamestown; communicated and traded with the Powhatans (e) interested in settlers; may have saved John Smith's life

2. They farmed, fished, and hunted.

3. They thought they would find gold and a passage to the Pacific Ocean.

4. The land was swampy, the water was bad, and it was hot in summer and cold in winter.

5. (a) British company that sponsored Jamestown trip; did not plan it well (b) boys who worked on sailing ships that brought settlers to Jamestown (c) farmers who grew food the settlement needed (d) 1609-1610, the year when Jamestown didn't have enough food

6. They were "gentlemen" and lacked survival skills.

7. Powhatan provided food and traded with John Smith; later he turned on the settlement and laid siege to it, nearly starving all the settlers.

8. He was badly hurt in an accident and returned to England.

9. Responses should mention learning to build, farm, and hunt more effectively and getting along with the Powhatans.

10. The first settlers chose a spot they could defend against the Spanish and reach by sailing up the river. Since Jamestown was on a peninsula, the Indians were easily able to lay siege to it and cut the settlers off from the mainland hunting grounds.

CHECK-UP 2

1. (a) Early governors of Jamestown: De la Warr kept the colonists there, and Dale moved the settlement to Henrico. (b) They married and had a child; went to England together, but Pocahontas died before they could return to Virginia. For a time, their marriage kept peace between Powhatans and colonists. (c) Opechancanough planned to massacre the settlers; Chanco warned some settlers, saving their lives.

2. A hurricane nearly prevented new colonists from reaching Jamestown.

3. (a) people who worked for 4-7 years for the person who paid their fare to the New World (b) first colonial representative government (c) crop that made the Virginia colony prosperous

4. Responses should include her carefree childhood as the Powhatan's favorite daughter, her protection of John Smith, her kidnapping and conversion, marriage and celebrity in England as Lady Rebecca.

5. He complained of its smell and its harm to the brain and lungs.

6. Tobacco planting required a lot of labor. Indentured servants were free after a certain number of years, and planters didn't want to keep paying for more servants. Slaves were forced to stay on the plantation.

7. Slavery means people are bought and sold as if they were property, and they are made to work without pay. This contradicts the idea of freedom—of being allowed to do what you want to do.

8. Women came for the first time in large numbers; first elected lawmakers; slaves came for the first time; foreign colonists were given same rights as English settlers; English settlers could own land.

9. "Divine right" meant that God had given them the right to rule, and so they could do whatever they wanted.

10. (a) 1619 (b) 1622 (c) 1610

CHECK-UP 3

1. (a) second governor of the Pilgrims; kept a written record of arrivals (b) Wampanoag chief who made treaty of peace with Pilgrims (c) first Indian to meet Pilgrims; welcomed them in English and introduced them to Massasoit (d) Indian who taught Pilgrims to fish and plant corn (e) Puritan leader and lawyer, chosen to govern Massachusetts Bay Colony

2. (a) first place Pilgrims went seeking religious freedom, but came back because they wanted to maintain their culture (b) former Indian village where Pilgrims started a colony (c) place where first Puritans settled in America

3. (a) Official church of England; because of their disagreement with the established church, the Pilgrims and Puritans left England. (b) Agreement among Puritans on how to organize colony; it showed the Pilgrims' intention to live under a government of laws. (c) Willingness to allow differences; the lack of toleration in England forced Pilgrims and Puritans to leave; Puritans denied toleration to others in America. (d) Puritan assembly that elected governor and council; it established a partially democratic government in New England.

4. Pilgrims believed they had to separate completely from the Church; Puritans wanted to remain in it but change (purify) it.

5. (a) government in which you choose someone else to vote for you (b) government in which you vote directly, without a representative (c) government by dictator (d) government by group of privileged people

6. They wanted everyone to be able to read the Bible.

7. It was not a theocracy, in which church leaders rule the people. In Massachusetts Bay Colony, ministers did not hold office.

8. Students may respond positively to the friendliness and communal aspects (shared grazing land; school; church) of a New England colonial village and negatively to the drawbacks of constant supervision by Puritan authorities, public punishments, required school, and all-day church services.

9. Many people of different views are leaving England for the colonies. They will not be content with Puritan punishments for long.
10. (a) Both (b) Puritans (c) Pilgrims (d) Pilgrims (e) Both (f) Both

CHECK-UP 4

1. (a) Puritan who believed in toleration; banished from Massachusetts; founded Rhode Island (b) Puritan who was banished from Massachusetts for challenging Puritan leaders (c) judge in Salem witchcraft trial who later apologized (d) Wampanoag leader who fought against colonial expansion and mistreatment (e) Pueblo leader who succeeded in driving Spanish out of New Mexico
2. Farming was easier in the fertile river valley than in rocky Massachusetts.
3. (a) freedom to do what you believe is right, rather than what others tell you is right—Quakers and some Puritans for; most Puritans against (b) swearing loyalty to a ruler or government—Puritans for; Quakers against (c) ruler's authority comes from God—Puritans for; Quakers against
4. (a) Where hangings took place; many people who disagreed with Puritans, such as Quaker Mary Dyer, were hung in Massachusetts. (b) The definition of a married woman that said she belonged to her husband; married women who questioned Puritan leaders defied this definition. (c) Forced to leave Massachusetts; a punishment handed down by the court to people who disagreed with the Puritans.
5. *Puritans:* women were chattel, and they had to be silent in church. *Quakers:* women were equal and participated in meetings.
6. Responses should show an understanding of mass hysteria during the Salem witch trials.
7. (a) War in Connecticut over land; in 1637, Pequots were almost completely wiped out by settlers. (b) Ended over 50 years of peace between Wampanoag and colonists; King Philip and Indian allies fought against spread of settlements in 1675-1676; were defeated by settlers in a vicious war. (c) Popé united tribes in New Mexico to successfully drive out the Spanish. After 12 years the alliance of tribes was weakened and the Spanish returned.
8. European settlers believed in clearing and owning land. Indians believed in preserving land and wildlife; land was to be shared, not owned.
9. The Pueblos suffered under the Spanish, who forced them to give up their religion and become Christians; eventually, the Pueblos united with other tribes to force the Spanish to leave. Wampanoags kept peace with settlers for over fifty years until eventually land disputes led to war.
10. (a) Massachusetts Bay (b) Plymouth (c) Rhode Island (d) Connecticut (e) New Haven (f) New Hampshire (g) Maine

CHECK-UP 5

1. (a) Dutch leader of New Netherland (b) leader of New Sweden (c, d) friends of the Duke of York who became proprietors of New Jersey (e) Quaker who founded Pennsylvania colony on Quaker ideals
2. New Netherland, New York, New Jersey
3. (a) animal pelts sold to Europeans for use as clothing and blankets (b) Dutch farm owner (c) owner of colonies
4. (a) Leader of the Puritans in Civil War; took over government after Charles I was beheaded; became a tyrant destroyed Anglican churches, closed theaters. (b) his beheading launched era of Puritan rule (c) supporters of the king, who found admirers in Southern Colonies (d) supporters of Cromwell, who found admirers in New England
5. Charles II gave land in America to his brother (New York) and others who had remained loyal during Puritan rule, which promoted growth of colonies.
6. Both granted freedom of religion and representative government
7. He encouraged freedom of conscience, equality, and toleration and respect for others, including Indians.
8. Responses should mention his desire for self-improvement, his curiosity, and willingness to work hard.
9. Diversity of people means different ideas and different skills; people learned from one another, causing change in how things were done.
10. Map should have colonies correctly labeled.

CHECK-UP 6

1. (a) founded Maryland (b) led a colonial rebellion in North Carolina (c) were pirates
2. Valuable crops like tobacco, rice, and indigo needed lots of workers, which led to importation of slaves from Africa and the West Indies and the growth of the economy and the population of Southern Colonies. Fertile farmland also attracted yeoman farmers to the Southern Colonies.
3. (a) Maryland's religious freedom act applied only to Christians. (b) It was supposed to encourage whites and Indians to trade and provide education to Indians, but many opposed it. (c) These were unpopular taxes imposed by England on trade between colonies.
4. (a) a person, often young, who worked unpaid for an employer for a set period of time, often learning a trade and getting room and board (b) plant from which blue dye is made; grown in South Carolina (c) language made up of words from African languages, English, and French, developed by African-Americans in South Carolina and still spoken today
5. Responses should note the privileged life and education of plantation owners' children, the hard work and lack of schooling for yeoman farmers, the possibility of harsh treatment of indentured servants, and the restrictions on the enslaved child.

6. North Carolina, Maryland, Virginia

7. Responses will vary.

8. The Southern colonies had closer ties to England, plantations, one- or two-crop agriculture, dependence on slavery.

9. They said it was unfair to pay taxes to England on goods they sold to other colonies.

10. (a) South Carolina (b) North Carolina (c) Virginia (d) Maryland

CHECK-UP 7

1. (a) English king who tried to take charge of the colonies, claimed divine right, lost power during Glorious Revolution. (b) African boy from Benin who was captured and sold as slave, wrote an autobiography that gives insight into the slave trade. (c) Idealist who founded Georgia as a colony for debtors to get a new start. (d) Most famous American frontiersman, explored beyond the Appalachian Mountains and led settlers through Cumberland Gap.

2. The mountains were difficult to cross, and were a barrier to settlers who wanted to move west.

3. (a) top of mountain range, from where rivers flow east to the Atlantic or west to the Mississippi (b) passageway through the mountains; made westward travel easier (c) 300-mile Indian trail that Daniel Boone took through the mountains; eventually became one of the main routes through the Appalachians

4. (a) ruled by a governor appointed by the king (b) owned by individuals (c) charter allowed colonists to govern themselves with an elected assembly and governor

5. It brought them closer to the idea of government by the people.

6. Georgia

7. The best land in the East was taken.

8. Responses will vary.

9. Paragraphs should indicate that the English government wanted the settlers to stay out of the western lands because it didn't want to have to build forts and defend the settlers, whereas the colonists wanted to take advantage of the rich farmland in the West.

10. *Royal:* New Hampshire, Massachusetts, New York, New Jersey, Virginia, North Carolina, South Carolina, Georgia; *Self-governing:* Rhode Island, Connecticut; *Proprietary:* Pennsylvania, Maryland, Delaware

RESOURCE 1

Question Chart for use throughout the book.

RESOURCE 2

1. Appalachian Mountains, Adirondack Mountains; 3,200–6,600 feet

2. Much of the Southern Colonies are low and flat. There is much land that is good for farming.

3. People traveling westward had to cross the Appalachian Mountains, which were high and rugged.

RESOURCE 3

Students will complete the chart with details from the book.

RESOURCE 4

1. The English traded with the Powhatan for corn.

2. Wahunsonacock suspected that the English really wanted to take the Powhatans' land.

3. Wahunsonacock, although a "savage," was courteous to the English.

4. Wahunsonacock desired peace between his people and the English, and was disappointed at how the English repaid the Powhatans' kindness to them.

RESOURCE 5

1. Many of the first settlers died and the colony almost failed because the settlers were unprepared for life in Virginia.

2. Responses will vary.

3. armor

4. Everybody in the family would be working to ensure their survival.

RESOURCE 6

1. Indians inhabit land that colonists claim and want to settle.

2. Many more colonists settled in New England, taking up more land and pushing the Indians out.

3. The colonists' settlements had not yet reached their lands.

RESOURCE 7

1. These paragraphs say that neither Wampanoags nor Pilgrims will hurt each other or steal each other's tools.

2. If either Wampanoags or Pilgrims were attacked by somebody else, they would come to each other's aid.

3. It would ensure that neither side would appear to be warlike toward the other.

4. Possible response: As more European settlers arrive, they will want to take over more of the Wampanoags' land, which will cause hard feelings.

RESOURCE 8

Paragraphs will vary but should be complete summaries of Rowlandson's experience.

RESOURCE 9

Students should label all 13 colonies correctly and draw clear boundaries between the New England, Middle, and Southern Colonies.

RESOURCE 10

1. Virginia; 35,000
2. 1730; 114,000
3. Virginia; 180,000
4. 1710

RESOURCE 11

Responses will vary but should be based on sound reasoning.

RESOURCE 12

Students' bar graphs should correctly correspond to the data in the table.

RESOURCE 13

Students will complete the chart with details from the book.

RESOURCE 14

Degrees of latitude and longitude are approximate.
1. 39° N 77° W 2. 36° N 106° W 3. 43° N 74° W 4. 39° N 121° W 5. 30° N 97° W 6. 47° N 101° W

RESOURCE 15

1. Delaware 2. Georgia 3. New Jersey 4. Rhode Island 5. Maryland 6. North Carolina 7. Pennsylvania 8. Virginia 9. New Hampshire 10. Connecticut 11. South Carolina 12. Massachusetts 13. New York

CPSIA information can be obtained
at www.ICGtesting.com
Printed in the USA
BVHW021735170723
667296BV00003B/7